NOW OR NEVER

To
Cliff

Best Wishes

[signature]

20/5/2015

NOW OR NEVER

BY TONY APPLETON

Text Gemma Appleton, on behalf of Story Terrace

Design Grade Design, London

Copyright © Tony Appleton & Story Terrace

Text is private and confidential

First print Sept 2016

www.StoryTerrace.com

CONTENTS

INTRODUCTION

Welcome to the story of my life. I do hope you learn a little more about the real person behind the personality who pops up every now and again on your TV, radio or newspaper, in this my autobiography. It is not meant to be in chronological order, but a collection of my treasured memories, shared for the first time.

Over the course of my 80 years, I've had dozens of jobs, the key ones being Carpet Salesman, Care Home Proprietor, Toastmaster and Royalist Town Crier. I'm really a Jack-of-all-trades. As they say, salesmen are born, not made. I have learned over the years that self-promotion is the key to success, and if you want something in this world, it's now or never!

Helen Rollason MBE

HELEN ROLLASON
CHARITY

Helen Rollason was the first female sports presenter on BBC's Grandstand. She fought an inspirational two-year battle with cancer, losing her valiant fight at the age of 43 on August 9, 1999. Profits from this book will go to support the very important work of the charity that was founded in her honour.

Enabling quality of life while living with cancer

The Helen Rollason Cancer Charity is dedicated to championing quality of life for everyone living with or affected by cancer. We are here to support men and women with all types of cancer at all stages: newly diagnosed, throughout and post treatment, as well as their wider support network of family, friends and carers. We do this through the provision of support centres, complementary therapies, information and advice and awarding grants for clinical trials. Our services are delivered free of charge to support cancer patients' emotional well-being alongside their medical treatment. We focus on offering these services in non-clinical environments to promote a safe, peaceful, relaxing setting across the Essex, London and Hertfordshire regions.

We are very grateful to Tony for his support of the Helen Rollason Charity.

Angela Lodge – HRCC

1. BEGINNINGS

MUM'S FAVOURITE

I was born on September 23, 1936, to Dolly (née Hawes) and Dick Appleton. They named me Anthony and I was their second child, a surprise if you will, my sister June being eleven years older than me. We lived at 66, Molrams Lane, Great Baddow, a pretty Essex village near the city of Chelmsford.

I was baptised at St John the Baptist Church, Danbury, at the same time as another baby. The father of the other baby was a British Army Officer, who had brought water back from the River Jordan to baptise his son. Some of that same water was used in my baptism, and I have always wondered if this accounted for me wanting to travel the world by sea. That day I was presented with a silver spoon – so I really was born with a silver spoon in my mouth!

Even though June was the spitting image of our dear mother, I was Mum's favourite, being a boy. I could never do anything wrong in Mum's eyes. When I was about four years old, Mum asked June to babysit me. She was unhappy,

Myself and My Sister June, 1955

because she and her friend wanted to go out. After Mum gave her a stern look, June agreed, and she and her friend took me to the Army and Navy pub, Chelmsford. After they'd had a few drinks, they left the pub, forgetting to take me with them! June got in serious trouble when Mum found out.

My father, an extremely tall man with a full head of hair, was very laid back. He was known as 'Danbury Dick' because he used to drive the bus up and down Danbury Hill. Dad was also called 'Ten-minute Dick' because it used to take him 10

My lovely mother Dolly, when she was 17

The Appleton family - Dolly, Richard, June   *My father Richard Appleton, aged 72*
and yours truly, 66, Molrams Lane,
Gt Baddow, 1946

minutes longer than any other bus driver to get his bus all the way up to the top of Danbury Hill where his parents ran the pretty Bell public house.

My paternal grandfather had terribly high blood pressure, which there was no cure for back in those days. He committed suicide before I was born, having been racked by pain and depression. Dad used to stop in and see my grandmother at the pub every night after he finished work as a bus driver.

One evening, halfway through his shift at Danbury, he was in a bad accident involving a motorbike. The bike came chasing down Danbury Hill, and went crashing head on into his bus, resulting in the motorcyclist and pillion being decapitated. When the Police arrived, they looked over the scene and spoke to witnesses. The Police quickly saw that it wasn't Dad's fault, so he was allowed to drive home. That incident scarred his mind for a long time.

Soon after this, Mum found out that Dad was flirting big time with a bus conductress. In a fury, Mum went looking all over Chelmsford for her, and eventually found her stepping off a bus at Chelmsford Bus Station. I watched from afar as Mum walked right up to the woman and slapped her round the face, which put a stop to that nonsense. Mum was not one to be messed about.

My father only had three jobs in his entire life – a lot different to me. His first job was as a sales representative. Then he worked as a bus driver for 30 years until he got dermatitis, which prevented him from working around oily engines. His last job was at the water mill at Sandford Mill. I remember that my Mum, bless her heart, used to boss him around something rotten. She was a kind lady, but she was completely in charge of our family.

SCHOOL DAYS

As a boy I attended Great Baddow Primary School. My mother worked at the school as a dinner lady. Having your Mum's eyes watching you while you desperately want to mess around with your friends at lunchtime isn't easy, but I suppose that did keep me in order. One of the teachers at the school was called Mr Cook, a short, dumpy man. He and I didn't get along at first. Back in the day, as everyone knows, teachers used to punish children by whacking them with a cane.

One day at school – I forget now what I had done – Mr Cook brought me up in front of the class. To teach me a lesson, he struck me with the cane so hard and so many times that Mum had to take me to the doctor's surgery after school. My injuries were quite severe. I was covered in bruises, and Mr Cook nearly got the sack over it. By way of an apology, he bought me some boxing gloves, thinking that would calm the situation down. Mr Cook had really taken it out on me; I remember it took me a while to trust him again. Eventually we became friends.

After that, Dad bought me a brand new bicycle, which I rode every day to school. One day, a local Policeman – who I think must have been off his trollop – saw me riding by on my brand new bike, and he pulled me over. He was a tall man who towered above me, which frightened me something rotten. He accused me of stealing the bike, so he took me back to his home station where I waited for three hours until he got hold of my father, who explained it was in fact my bike. That annoyed me a lot at the time, as I knew I hadn't done anything wrong, and I was missing boxing club for no reason.

I was a popular boy at school. I had a good following of mates by my side, and throughout my life, I have had good mates. I have also always liked to keep busy. Some of my earliest memories are of the jobs I used to do as a child. From cleaning chicken sheds out at Molrams Lane, to running paper rounds in mornings, I always had a job. Money gave me the independence to do my own thing, and I loved being able to buy whatever I wanted. As a child, my parents used to give me a little pocket money, but I topped it up with whatever I could earn from the farm. I always wanted to be my own boss, not to have anyone to answer to. Even today, approaching 80, I still want to make my own decisions and work hard to earn the rewards.

BLUE SKIES AND SHOTGUNS

My summer holidays were spent at Bargate Farm in Dedham, which was owned by one of my many uncles. Mum used to pack me off for six weeks every year. Even though we were close, I could be a mischief-maker, so I'm sure she looked forward to me going away for the summer. At the farm, I was always outside. My uncle Stan Hawes, who had a farm at East Hanningfield, owned a bunch of successful racehorses, the best being Zip Goes A Million and Truthful Dianna. He

bought Zip from George Formby, a famous actor at the time, who sang *When I'm Cleaning Windows*. Those two horses in particular won a lot of races, and I was always very proud of that.

One hot summer, while out shooting rabbits with my cousin, something terrible happened. My uncle had let us go out with a shotgun that we hadn't realized was loaded, a misstep that he greatly regretted afterwards. As I climbed through a hole in a fence, the gun caught on a branch and went BANG, narrowly missing my cousin's face. They wouldn't let us use the gun again.

I had another uncle on my father's side who also owned a farm. When I was old enough, I worked in the hop fields, helping out and getting paid peanuts in return. I would work on those fields all day long for six weeks every summer, and come back to school feeling energized and sun-kissed. They were my unforgettable summer holidays, earning money and getting into mischief.

I've always fancied myself a performer and, at school, I would always be singing up and down the corridors in break time. I loved to make people laugh, and really enjoyed telling a good story. My friends would always ask me to tell them stories because I had a vivid imagination. I could act out different voices, and they loved that. I remember that children would gather around and listen to me telling stories. We would

The happy reaper at Bargate Farm, Dedham, 1948

sometimes get told off for not hearing the school bell. Maybe that was what annoyed Mr Cook that day with the cane?

I remember finding a half-finished canoe one day at the school, so I asked my teacher if I could finish building it. I taught myself the necessary carpentry skills, and finally got it finished and in good working order. My friends and I would take it to the River Chelmer, where we splashed around until our mothers called us back for tea time. That must have been one of the first projects I saw through and, since then, I have always enjoyed teaching myself new skills.

In the playground, when I wasn't storytelling, you would have found me engaging in a bit of rough and tumble. So, when I was old enough, my father allowed me to join Chelmsford Boxing Club to expel some of that boyish energy. I would spend most of my evenings as a young teenager there, sparring around with other boys my age. In the years after leaving the Royal Navy, I used some of the tricks I learned in Boxing Club in real life, which is not something I am hugely proud of, but it did come in handy.

FRIENDS AND FOES

At the age of 12 my friends and I moved up from Great Baddow Primary School to Moulsham Secondary School. I still see some of my old school friends and foes around the village today. I was fairly well behaved at Moulsham Secondary, but I always stood up for myself in situations where it was necessary.

I remember there was a nasty boy at school called John. He had it in for me from the start, and used to try and bully me all the time. I was terrified of him. One day, I had had enough of him picking on me, and decided to retaliate. I stormed up to him and knocked him straight out. From that day, I was the toughest kid at school; I had become the king of the castle. Years later, John and I became mates and all was forgotten about.

All in all, I had a happy childhood. I was always outside, doing jobs to try and earn some extra pocket money. During my years at Secondary School, I attended a night school to learn the skills of being a carpenter. One foggy night, I made my way home on my bicycle. Unbeknown to me, somebody had shut the yard gates. In the fog I couldn't see well, and I smashed right into them, knocking both of my flipping front teeth out. I was in hospital for about a fortnight, it was horrible. After that accident, I was called 'gummy' at school. Throughout the Royal Navy, I had to wear a plate in my mouth, which I sometimes lost. As the years progressed, I've gone back and forth to the dentist, but now have implants, which serve me well.

CHOIR BOY

I had a Christian upbringing and, as a young boy, I used to attend St Andrew's Church at Sandon. My father was a sides man and our family was heavily involved in church life. Before bedtime, Mum would always make me say my prayers, which I still do to this day.

I was even in the church choir for a little while. I always loved to sing, and maybe that's where I got my passion for performing. I had no problems performing in front of large crowds, and at home I remember I would practice singing in the mirror, which made Mother think I was mad.

I remember the vicar at the church sometimes carried the services out under the oak tree, and one time he recited the Lord's Prayer in Japanese. I recall asking him where he learned the language and he told me he had been imprisoned in a Japanese POW camp for years. Listening to him praying in a foreign language really inspired me to travel the world.

2. A PIRATE'S LIFE FOR ME

Mum knew the Headmaster at Great Baddow Primary School, and she persuaded him to let me take a Grammar School entrance exam. I knew I wouldn't pass because I had never been very good at academics. I failed the entrance exam with flying colours. My mother had wanted me to have an education, but after this she decided it might be a good idea for me to get an apprenticeship instead.

At the age of 12 I joined Chelmsford Sea Cadets. I knew I wanted to join the Royal Navy, so this seemed to be the best step towards making that dream a reality. As a young child, I always wanted to be a pirate. When I was old enough I frequently visited the local cinema to watch films about pirates and the Royal Navy. I knew after watching those films that I had to be a sailor. Going way back in our family history, there is a rumour that the Appletons were pirates. Maybe it's true because I had an obsession for the sea!

My father knew a guy who worked at Sandford Mill waterworks. He was a prisoner-of-war, and he used to take me down to Baddow Meads where he taught me how to swim. Because I knew how to swim, one of the jobs I took after leaving the Royal Navy was head pool attendant at Chelmsford swimming pool.

After I left Moulsham School, my mother arranged for me to go to an interview at Chalks Farm in Howe Green. The job involved building chicken sheds. I got the job, but only stayed there for one year. An old boy who worked there was a retired soldier, and he would always talk to me about his days in the British Army, recounting all the fun he used to have abroad. I used to listen intently; his stories of being overseas fascinated me. After talking to him, I decided I wanted to see the world, and made it my mission to join the Royal Navy. I could be a sailor *and* travel the world – bliss!

AHOY THERE!

At the age of 17 I came home from my job building chicken sheds at Howe Green, and announced to my parents that I wanted to join the Royal Navy. This news did not go down well with my father. He flew into a rage – he wouldn't have it. When he eventually calmed down, he advised me that I would have to sign up for 21 years, and that I would regret my decision. We had so many arguments about me joining the Navy, and I was furious because he was trying to stop me.

The following week, I took myself into Chelmsford on my own steam, ignoring my father's advice. I walked straight into the building on Wells Street to sign up for the Royal Navy, and was told I would have to sit an entrance test. I wasn't very good at maths or academics, and, unsurprisingly, I failed the test. The old recruiting officer told me to come back again, so the next day I went back and re-sat the test. Again, I failed.

The officer could see how much I wanted to be in the Navy, so he let me through anyway. I went bounding home and shouted to Mum, "I've only got into the Navy!" to which Dad replied, "Well, I'm not signing it." I couldn't believe my ears. There was absolute hell to pay in the house after that. It was an absolute nightmare to persuade him, but in the end, Mum talked him round into signing the papers. I've often thought about why he didn't want me to sign up. My Dad and I weren't really close for whatever reason, bless his heart. I remember one time I upset my Dad, and he chased me all over the fields in front of our house hitting me with a slipper.

Now I am older and wiser I realise Dad was worried how my mother would cope if something untoward happened if I saw action on the High Seas.

I remember clearly when, on the day before I left for the Royal Navy, Uncle Bill took me to one side. It must have been my mother's idea to have this chat with me, because I could sense she was listening in from the next room. Uncle Bill told me all about the birds and the bees, and told me how to be careful about not catching venereal disease while abroad. An invaluable lesson, indeed!

FIRST LOVE

Never in my life had I travelled abroad until I joined the Royal Navy, so receiving my first passport was a momentous occasion. The first trip was to Hong Kong, via Singapore. I was so excited about going; I remember I had my bags packed weeks before we left. I dearly missed my parents while I was away. We always wrote and sent letters to each other. I loved the Navy, but at the beginning I cried to come home out of homesickness. I remember I had two weeks to make my mind up, but I soon decided I would stick it out when I met Lucille. She was a girl from British Guiana – and what a catch she was!

My first posting in the Royal Navy was on troopship MV Cheshire. We travelled from Southampton to Hong Kong, with the first stop being at Singapore. It was on that journey that I met Lucille. She was a nurse stationed in the British Army. Lulu had the most infectious personality, and she loved to talk to me about her adventures being an Army nurse. We fell in love, becoming besotted with each other in that short six-week trip.

The perfume she wore used to drive me around the bend, and I remember finding it incredibly frustrating that we could never find a moment alone on board the ship to sneak a kiss. If we were caught, we would have both been chucked off, so

The youngest sailor aboard HMS Constance wearing the Chief Petty Officer's rig on Christmas Day 1954, as the Captain's was too large!

MV Cheshire, 1954

we had to be very careful. Maybe that's what was so appealing about Lulu, the secrecy around our relationship drove me mad. From getting into the Royal Navy, to becoming a salesman later on, I have always had a drive to achieve the impossible.

Lulu had to disembark at our first port of call, Singapore. I remember feeling empty without her, but knew somehow I would see her again. When the ship left Singapore and we were on our way to Hong Kong, my crew were caught in a terrible typhoon. I have never seen anything like it. The waves tossed the ship around in the water, and we all feared for our lives as lightning filled the sky. Thankfully, we made it to the shores of Hong Kong soon enough and dried off quickly.

Lovely Lulu and Junior Seaman Appleton sightseeing in Aden, 1954

After Lulu and I had said our goodbyes at Singapore, we kept in touch with each other by writing letters. Upon arriving into Hong Kong, I received a letter from her telling me that luck was on our side, and that her ship was on its way to Hong Kong. The moment should have been one filled with joy, but instead, I felt glum. We had been told that morning that our ship was going home to England, so it was too late to see each other again. Our ships literally passed each other in the water; we missed each other by only an hour.

All was not bad, however. Lulu got a job as a nurse in London, so when she came to England of course I hurriedly went to meet her. At that time, I was the Captain's chauffeur on my last ship, the HMS Bermuda, a cruiser, and I used to escort officers to golf clubs in the Land Rover. I had been given a mission to drive the Land Rover from Portsmouth, and they gave me a three-day period in which to do it. Along the way, I stopped off at Lulu's house in London. Because Lulu was foreign, my friends felt a bit strange about us being together. My Mother wasn't too happy about it either, but we were determined to show everyone how much we loved one another.

I arrived at her house in London, and was greeted by the beautiful Lulu at the door. Unbeknown to me, shortly after the time I had known her on the ship, she had fallen pregnant by an Indian Army Officer. When she opened the door holding a baby, she immediately saw the worried look on my face. Lulu quickly told me not to worry, that she was only looking after the baby for a friend. When she went out to the shop to buy the baby some milk, I found a letter on the mantelpiece, which was all about her baby. I discovered the truth – that the baby was hers – and feeling slightly distraught, I left while she was out. All along she had been leading me up the garden path. I was 19 and she broke my heart!

THE NAVY LARK

One of my favourite warships was HMS Constance, but I very nearly sank her with a screwdriver. She was at Chatham Dockyard for maintenance and I had to go into the bilge, right at the bottom of the hull to clean her up. Me and a mate were on painting punishment, so we were using red lead paint and the fumes were horrible.

I told my mate in a jokey fashion: "I'm going to sink this ship!" I held a screwdriver to the steel hull and hit it with a hammer, to my horror the screwdriver went right through a rusty piece and the ship sprung a leak. We both ran for it up the ladders, as it was beginning to look like we had hit an iceberg. We never told a soul and they never found out who done it. After this it wasn't long before dear old Constance was razor blades.

ICEBERGS, TORPEDOES AND EXCUSES

Being at sea, our ship would pass all the sights the Seven Seas had to offer. Porpoises and dolphins would follow our ship along, and surprise us all by jumping out of the water to say hello. One time, after dropping a load of depth charges into the water, we saw millions of dead fish float to the surface. That was a sight I'll never forget.

I once asked my Petty Officer if he had ever been in trouble while in the Navy, and he replied, "I've got 25 years of

Riding an elephant in the ancient kingdom of Kandy, Sri Lanka, formerly Ceylon, 1955

undetected crime, Appleton." It was one of those sayings that I still use today before I embark on a gate-crashing mission. I only ever got in trouble once during my time in the Royal Navy for being late, due to my train being delayed. The officers did not take that as an excuse, and so I had to stand before the Commander at Chatham Barracks. Behind the Commander on the wall was a list of all the excuses written up in gold leaf on a board that you could think of for being late. If you could think of an excuse that wasn't on the list, they would let you off. Of course, train delay was at the top of that list, so that was the only time I got into trouble. Once a Navy man, you never lose the discipline of time, and even to this day I cannot be late anywhere.

During my time at Chatham Barracks, us young sailors used to hang around with an old 'three-badge' sailor. He used to give me a load of perks, such as drinks and time off. One day, he brought me to his office and shut the door. He tried to get a hold of me, and chased me around his office. I did not appreciate his intentions whatsoever, and I ran out of there as quick as lightning. I should have realized why he was giving me all those perks!

I had many good mates in the Royal Navy, but like in any place, you can't expect to get along with everyone. 'Stripey' Millgate used to bully me like hell. I can see him now with his false teeth. Every night, before he went to bed, he would take them out and put them on the fan shaft above his bed. One night I crept in, grabbed his teeth and threw them over the side of the ship. For the whole rest of the journey he had no teeth, but nobody ever found out who did it. Sweet revenge.

Because I used to do shift work, I was the only boy on the ship who was allowed all-night leave. I would go ashore and come back the next day as you might say. I won't tell you what I got up to! One night I was on board keeping a lookout when a load of incredibly drunk crew came back from shore. They decided they had it in for me, maybe because I was the youngest boy on the ship. They started on me, and kicked me around the ship like a football. I was battered and bruised, but I got over it.

On Sundays I used to like taking a quick afternoon nap, which I still do, and one day, as I was snoozing away, a torpedo went off and blasted through the bulkhead next to my room. It left a huge hole right by my bed. That certainly woke me up, although it never went off.

Another hairy part of my naval life was time I spent in Cyprus attached to the lifeguards. One of our missions was to take the terrorist flags off of the roofs of the buildings. I asked my Petty Officer at the time if I could keep a flag as a souvenir, and he said yes, but told me to be careful getting one because it might be wired. I got on top of the school roof, shut my eyes, and pulled the flag up! It was a very risky thing

What crisis? Taking my customary afternoon kip aboard HMS
Diamond on the Suez Canal

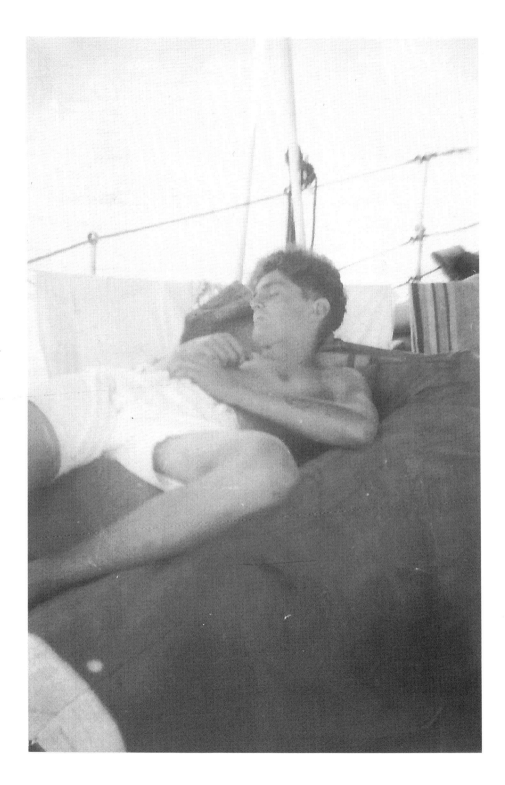

to do, and when I left the Royal Navy, I used to take it to all my parties.

Another time that I got away with getting into trouble was when we were in Italy. Our ship had landed at Sicily, and my mates and I went out for the evening. After a few drinks, we got into a fight with some locals. The Police arrested us and escorted us back to the ship. One of the officers tried to steal the ring off my finger, but because we made such a fuss about that they didn't bother to tell our commander that we had been arrested.

KOREAN WAR

During the signing of the armistice, we were stationed in the port of Nagoya, Japan. One of my fellow comrades was desperate to get out of the Royal Navy, and one morning he clambered onto the deck, hauling along the Soviet Union flag with him. He stood up and waved the Red Flag around like a madman. All the Yanks quickly pulled out their guns on him and he later got slung out of the Royal Navy.

Another friend of mine acted deaf to try and get out of the Navy, so he tried his luck at getting his ticket out. He stood in front of the Commanding Officer – I can remember it like it was yesterday – they questioned him, and he pretended that he couldn't hear a thing. He held his hands to his ears to show them he couldn't hear their questions. He got through the whole interview pretending to be deaf. As he walked out of the room at the end of the interview, they asked him to close the door behind him, which he of course did. That was him done – he was in serious trouble after that for lying.

After the signing of the armistice, we travelled to Iceland. During our posting we were instructed to blow up an iceberg. Even in those days it was some serious money to use a torpedo, but we had to do it as a practice. The crew went on deck to fire the torpedo, including the Captain, and we were all standing at attention when BANG, the torpedo fired. The skipper must have been having a bad hair day because the torpedo missed the huge iceberg. Torpedoes eventually surface to water, and we picked it up about a week later.

We left Iceland, and I went to Portsmouth to do an 18-month gunnery course. That was a tough time; the course leaders were so hard on everyone. One day I was cycling across the parade ground at our Whale Island base when a Petty Officer shouted: "Pick that bike up and run with it!" so I did just that, as it was a very strict regime. One time, I had to return home four times because they said my hair was not cut short enough. The Chief Petty Officer at the time was called Alan White and, unbeknown to me, he came from Great Baddow. Years later I bumped into him in the King's Head public house in our village. I suddenly recognised him at the bar and called out: "Don't you recognise me, it's Able Seaman Appleton with his haircut!" CPO White had been responsible for sending me home and there we were sharing a pint and talking Navy.

A RUM JOB

There were perks to being based in Portsmouth. I was lucky enough to get a perk as a rum bosun, dishing out the rum. The rum that was left over was called sippers, which we were allowed to drink for free. I used to make sure we got a lot extra leftover by using a plastic measuring cup. I filed it down so it wasn't a correct measure, so I could get more of that leftover rum!

THE SUEZ CRISIS

After my gunnery course, we sailed for Tripoli, Libya. When the Suez Crisis started, we all had to get back onboard quickly because the locals were getting really aggravated about us being there. I remember messing about up a back street on my own, thinking I was movie tough guy Kirk Douglas. I was quite tough too. I can't remember now how it started, but I went into a carpenter's shop and this bloke challenged me to an arm-wrestling match. After I beat him he threw me on the floor. All the locals gathered around me. I thought they were going to have me, but I managed to scarper back to the ship. The locals started trying to push needles into our arms as we clambered to get back aboard. My mate swung round and knocked one of the Arab's teeth out, which we all got in trouble for and were ordered to pay for his new tooth.

I was serving on HMS Diamond, a frigate in Egypt, as a gunner. It was four in the morning. I remember it well. We were all prepared, and I got on a gun, having never fired a shot before. We were aiming for cover fire but I couldn't resist blowing the side off of the hotel ahead of us. The gunman on board immediately slung me off! The Egyptian Army started firing back at us – only little bullets – but we had to duck for cover. The Americans didn't want us to go in there, and their warplanes used to 'dive bomb' to scare us off.

One of the times – I remember it clearly – I was a bit of a naughty boy. I had this gunnery officer who really didn't like me; he gave me so much stick. We used to shoot practice fire, and this guy was in charge of the guns. I decided to put a live round in it. I shouldn't have done it, but I did anyways. BANG! Nobody could work out where the live round had come from. Sailors were questioned, and I claimed I had nothing to do with it. Eventually, the Gunnery Officer got demoted as punishment to Able Seaman. He never found out it was me, and a good thing too!

Often when on leave I would go to Boreham to see my friends. I was a big dancer back then. I would dance for so long that my friends used to call me 'rubber legs'. That nickname stuck with me for years. They also used to call me 'Scrumpy Appleton' because I really liked my cider. I was a huge Elvis fan and, in 1956, when Elvis kicked off his career, I can remember a Leading Seaman telling me that Elvis was a nobody and wouldn't go anywhere. He said that I would hear no more of him after his first song. How wrong he was!

We were later stationed in Greenland. It was a stunning landscape, but on most days, the mist was so bad that one minute you would see a ship ahead of you, and then if you turned your head for only five seconds, it was gone. The mist was so heavy that it would just suddenly drop. There were a couple of guys on board who decided to pinch a kayak one night after a few drinks on shore leave. When they tried to find our ship, they couldn't because the mist had dropped. They couldn't see us, and we couldn't see them. We never saw the men alive again. After a week, we found their bodies and buried them at sea.

BUYING MYSELF OUT

During my time in the Royal Navy, we docked in America, Bermuda, Cyprus, Egypt, Gibraltar, Greenland, Korea, Hong Kong, Iceland, Italy, Japan, Malta, Newfoundland, Sri Lanka and Singapore. I sailed the Seven Seas, living out my childhood dream.

I did everything I wanted to do in the Navy, but after seven years, I decided to buy myself out. I was a sailor, and had travelled the world, but it was time to start my next adventure. I had signed up for 21 years, but a scheme was created where you could buy yourself out. One day, when I was on leave, I walked into NatWest bank in Chelmsford, and I asked to see the bank manager. I told him I wanted a personal loan for £120 – a lot of money in those days. The bank manager had never heard anyone ask for a loan to buy themselves out, so he told me I would need to get a job in order for him to give me a loan. I went to Foreman's, in Rainsford Road, asked for a job, and then went straight back to the bank and told the manager I was employed.

It was when I was out in Greenland that the signal came through that I had been given the discharge. I never started my job at Foreman's as a carpenter. When I came home, I discovered I was partially deaf. I can remember when we were going along the Korean coast, and although the armistice was being signed, we were still firing at each other. The gunfire was so loud and in those days you weren't allowed to put your hands to your ears. When I returned home, I got compensation for the loss of hearing, which was a mere 50p per week. I then got offered a lump sum of £600, which was terrible, but I accepted it anyway.

3. FINDING THE RIGHT PATH

FIGHTS, SCRAPS AND SCUFFS

After leaving the Royal Navy, I became the black sheep of the family. I had so much discipline for the seven years I served that I started testing my boundaries. I found myself getting into a lot of trouble. On the evening of being de-mobbed, I was on the way home to Chelmsford. I got on the train and had a few drinks, as you do. I got invited to this compartment on the train by a bunch of French guys.

They too had been drinking. Then all of a sudden, they turned on me. Unbeknown to them, I was quite a fit lad, having just left the Royal Navy, and I duffed up three of them, breaking their noses. I opened the door of the slow-moving train, and jumped off, hiding in the bushes from the Police who were looking for me. I waited until the next train came along, and hopped on that, narrowly escaping jail. Thankfully the Police and those men never caught me.

On settling back into Chelmsford, I clued up as a bouncer at the Lion and Lamb public house nightclub. One night, I got attacked by three men who left me for dead. When I got home, Mum barely recognised me. She called the Police, who came round to question me. I said I had no idea who had attacked me, which was a lie. I chose then to get my revenge. I shouldn't have done it, but I hunted them down. I took each individual man on his own merit, and broke their noses. One of the men told the Police. We both got fined a fiver and we both avoided jail. That happened 50 years ago, but it is still on my record today.

THIRTY-SIX JOBS

Because of the discipline I had during the Royal Navy, I was a different person when I left. I stupidly got in with the wrong crowd, and got into lots of problems with the Police. I also couldn't decide on what job I wanted, which made my mum think that I would never be able to settle down. In between leaving and starting up Tony Appleton Carpets, I took up 36 different jobs. Some jobs were fantastic – others, not so.

Here is a list of my jobs: sweeping up at Hoffmann's ball-bearing factory, handing leaflets out, being a stock welder, a demolition worker, a pylon fixer, a coalman, a debt collector, a bus conductor, a security guard, a ground worker, a part-time postman, a steel erector, a bouncer, a diamond dredger, a Toastmaster, a photographer, a lorry driver, a carpenter, a market salesman for cushions, a carpet salesman, a potato seller, a diet food salesman, a rigger, a jewellery salesman, a water filters salesman, giving talks on the life of a Town Crier and Toastmaster, a carpet cleaner, a tragedy insurance broker, a burglar alarm salesperson, a removal company mover, a window cleaner, a karaoke DJ, a TV aerial erector, a chicken catcher and a hotel proprietor.

One of the first jobs I landed was at Marconi, New Street. I absolutely hated it. I had started the job in the morning, sweeping up the factory floor and, by lunchtime, I had thrown in the brush and gone home.

I also spent some time working as a demolition worker. One day, I was driving my tipper down the old A12 when I touched the wrong button on the controls. The crane went straight up in the air and pulled all the telephone wires down as I drove through Hatfield Peverel. Some bloke was watching TV when it happened, and it pulled all the wires from the side of his house off. Of course, I got the sack. Imagine all the traffic chaos around there!

During my time as a debt collector, I had to make a couple of phone calls to a man who owed one of my client's money. He refused to pay it back, so I kept calling, day after day. After a week, I discovered that this man was involved with the Kray Brothers, and they were after me. When I heard this I set off immediately to Heathrow Airport, knowing I had to get out of the country. The Krays weren't going to have the last laugh. I clued up in Johannesburg, and got a job as a steel erector.

I had never put up scaffolding in my life, so I ran away when they put me in charge of a work gang.

DIAMOND COAST

I got the train down to Cape Town, and got a job dredging for diamonds from a barge off German South-West Africa, now called Namibia. This really turned out to be my favourite job of all. It was so exciting, seeing the world and collecting diamonds! Me and the other guys flew an old Dakota, which had no air conditioning, and was freezing cold in the desert.

The Diamond Coast was guarded by ex-Nazi soldiers, who searched you in and searched you out when you came back from work. We used to take off on a helicopter to the barge where we spent one week off and two weeks on. The barge had a big pump, which sucked diamonds out from under the seabed.

One day we were flying over the dunes and just as we landed on the barge, the tail of the helicopter dropped off. If this had happened 10 seconds earlier, we would have all ended up in the sea. During my weeks off I used to visit the area of District 6 to have a late snifter. Nobody was allowed to go there; it was out of bounds, but I used to sneak there anyway. One day, while traveling to District 6, our car broke down, and everyone was worried. Thankfully, we got it fixed in time without getting caught.

CAPE FEAR

In Cape Town, I had a girlfriend. We used to have lunch together every Sunday. During that time, it was illegal to have a black girlfriend, so I would have to jump over the roofs to get to her house. The police heard what I was up to. They had these souped-up Italian-Job Minis, but they still couldn't catch me. The word on the block was that I could get six months for dating her, so I knew I had to get out of town, pronto. Having a black girlfriend, and being involved in a near helicopter crash made me think heck, I'm going to pack this up, so I came home on the Northern Cross cruise ship. I was making good money from being a diamond dredger, but it was too dangerous. I never got a chance to say goodbye to her.

The scariest job I found was when I was a steel erector. I lost my finger when I caught it in a winch. I was working night shifts in Wales, and we were greasing up masts on the boats. I didn't bring a winch up with me, so I called down below for someone to bring one up to me. I got bored of waiting because it took about half an hour for someone to get to the top. I started fiddling around with a bit of string on the throttle, and the string got caught in the fan. The end of my finger ripped off. The doctor tried to stitch it back together, but it fell straight off and into the bin. 'Oh my god!' I thought. He couldn't put it on after that.

ON THE BUSSES

It was a really close friend of mine, Terry Ledworth, who got me into bus conducting. He was my bus driver for a long time before I owned a car, and we became good mates. On the side, Terry would sell potatoes, which we did together to make some extra cash. During the summer season when there were no potatoes around, Terry asked me if I wanted to be his bus conductor. I happily agreed, and we started working together on bus routes around Chelmsford. He was the bus driver, and I was the bus conductor, working as a team.

One night, early on into our joint career, I had a date with a girl from the village. I couldn't switch the shift that Terry and I were working on and Terry, being such a good friend, let me go home early so I could go on the date! There must have been a lot of people left waiting for their bus that night!

Terry and I always used to muck around, and one day I literally just stepped off the bus at the bus station, and he drove off without me. Terry had a full busload of people, who were all in fits of laughter as he drove off. Both of us got the sack in the end. We were having a cup of tea in the bus canteen watching the football on TV when the boss came in and shouted that we had missed our first ride of the day. Our bus conducting/driving days were over – but we did have some real fun. A few years later, Terry got me into the world of carpets, and he then moved to America where he desperately tried to get me to go with him. I wasn't interested. Chelmsford was now my home.

4. A SALESMAN IS BORN

I've always believed that salesmen are born and not made, and when I left the Royal Navy, I discovered I was a salesman. I left Cape Town with £140 in my pocket, and I knew I needed to do something to keep the money coming in.

Terry Ledworth asked me to go with him to an interview at Cyril Lords, a big carpet sales company based in Chelmsford. I walked into the Blue Lion pub, and went up to my mate Harvey Dickson. I explained I had an interview as a Carpet Salesman. He said, "Don't forget to take your wellington boots with you." He truly believed that I could be nothing other than a ground worker. Well that really got up my back. I wanted to prove him wrong. I went to Ilford for the interview with Ray Mace. He wanted to show me how to go out cold canvassing – knocking on doors to sell carpets. I took the samples, and went round knocking on doors with him that evening. I had a natural talent for it and soon I started to excel in it. After making a good few sales, Ray gave me the job. I knew then that I was a salesman, and wanted to do nothing else with my life.

CHICK MAGNETS

Not long after starting, I was making mega bucks. I bought an
E-Type Jaguar for £3,300, which made me look the business.
The same day the E-type was delivered to my house, I had a
new van delivered. All my neighbours thought I had done a
bank robbery! I used to come back to the E-type after doing
my shopping in town and find notes written by ladies on the
windscreen asking me to call them. I also owned a replica Del
Boy three-wheeler car, which attracted fewer ladies as it was
decked out with Trotter's Independent Trading Co sign on

Morecambe and Wise at the Opening of Tony Appleton Carpets, mid-1960s

the side! My Reliant Robin blew up in the car park at Tesco; the fire brigade turned up and put it out. That caused some attention and again more publicity for me!

After a while, I became Cyril Lord's top salesman, and Ray Mace advised me that I should start up my own carpet shop. So, I took up a shop next to Woolworths in Chelmsford. Business thrived, so I set up another shop in Moulsham Street, and called it Tony Appleton Carpets. I did well there, and had comedy duo Morecambe and Wise come down and open my next shop in Market Road, which was featured on TV and all the newspapers. I then opened up a bedding shop called Tony Appleton Bedding, and another carpet shop.

My dear friend Les Cooper called me up and told me about this big store at Wilson's Corner, Brentwood, and we went in it together. Eric and Ernie came down to Chelmsford numerous times to open each shop and photographs of them larking around taken by *Essex Chronicle* snapper Ray Horsnall are featured on Flickr. I have always believed that if you don't feed the fish, you don't get a bite. You don't get anything unless you ask!

TONY PARTY ANIMAL

I left my parents' home at the age of 30. I bought my mother's house for her at Molrams Lane, which I paid £1,800 for. I sold it later on, and bought the house next door for her instead. I then bought a piece of land, and had my bungalow built, which is where I still live, 50 years later. It's like a living museum – with my celebrity photos, autographed books, DVDs and publicity-stunt souvenirs on display.

One of my favourite things to do in Chelmsford during my carpet bagging years was to throw big parties. It was a small room at the top of the carpet shop, but it used to get packed out. The whole town knew about my parties, and the Police were always coming around to tell us off for causing too much noise. We used to drink a lot, and stand around bad-talking.

Sometimes, we had strippers turn up too. One time, a stripper came up with a huge Alsatian as her guard dog. Once the parties got bigger, we moved them from my carpet shop to my bungalow.

People invited their friends, and they invited their friends, and soon everyone was talking about them. Saturday night was party night. We had music, drink and laughter. We might have had the odd fight, but not the evil things like you get today. Before the parties on a Saturday night, we used to go to the disco a lot, Duke's being the big favourite. After going to the club, everyone would end up at mine for more fun and drinks. I was once at a party in Maldon, and I was chatting to a pretty lady when her boyfriend came storming over.

We got into a fight and, taking me completely by surprise, he pulled out a gun and turned it on me. In a flash, I pulled the gun off him, hit him round the head with the back of it and ran off, taking the gun and his girlfriend with me. I met up with him two weeks later and gave it back to him. In those days, I was the party animal of the village!

THE FOUR MUSKETEERS

Let me tell you more about that very dear friend of mine, a lovely man called Les Cooper. We were so close, and we bought each other so many presents over the years. Les left me some money in his will, bless him, which was unexpected and very generous. He was so good to me. He knew I was a big Royalist, and he supported me in everything I wanted to do.

Together with chums Peter Bryant and Roy Parker we used to call ourselves the Four Musketeers. Amazingly we all met by chance at a pub one day when I was having a really rough day. I had just got off with a woman, and we had moved into a small flat together in Southend. I told her that I needed to pop out for a quick pint to check out the new local, and she said she would have lunch ready for me when I got home in 20 minutes.

She told me not to be late, and off I went. I got to the pub at 11:55. I joined the line of other fellas who were eagerly awaiting their pints. I saw Les in the line, and asked him how long until it opened. We got chatting, and after five minutes, we had a pint in our hands, chatting to the other guys in the group – Peter and Roy.

We all really hit it off that day, and just could not stop laughing and joking around. We ended up getting utterly drunk, and staggering back to our homes. I eventually turned up at our new pad, where my girlfriend was waiting with her lunch stone cold. She threw it at me, and stormed out, and I never saw her again! When I told Les that she had left me in the lurch, we had such a laugh. From then on the Four Musketeers became really close friends and used to meet at this Southend pub every Sunday.

WATCH IT, MATES

One year, Les and I went to Mexico. I always used to copy Les; I looked up to him a lot. Everything Les had, I had to have. Before our trip, we got flashy Rolex watches and we never took them off. I don't know how we got away with not having them nicked in Acapulco. Then when we were driving to Lake Tahoe in North America to go skiing, we stopped at a hotel on the Sierra Nevada border where Sinatra hung out. We were absolutely expecting to get mugged, and it was so strange that we did not. That night I made a bet to Les that I could persuade the lovely looking musician lady to let me sing a song. Les did not believe that I would go through with it. After chatting up the woman a bit, I got on stage. I looked into the crowd at the bar – bloody Les had buggered off to bed, and never paid the bet.

COOPER CLASS

On another trip, Les and I went to New York. He went by Concorde, of course. Les had a fair amount of cash, so we used to say that there was First Class, and there was Cooper Class. He used to roll cigarettes with a £50 note, all that sort of thing. So, Les flew in Cooper Class in his Concorde, and I went by scheduled. I arrived the day before Les, and as soon as we touched down in the airport, I arranged for a private helicopter to collect us to fly us into the city. When he arrived at the airport, I put out an announcement: "Les Cooper, will you meet Tony Appleton at the helicopter pad?" And so I arranged a pilot to fly us into New York. I wanted to one-up him!

We were there and so was John Lennon, but I was too busy to ask the Beatle for a photograph. Rather stupidly we used to walk through Central Park just to see if anyone would mug us of those Rolex! Les used to have a place in Majorca, and one day we had gone out for lunch, and we were in a taxi going back when the Police pulled in front of us. He had forgotten to pay the bill at the restaurant so we had to go back – just one of the scrapes we got up to and one example of why I miss him so much.

I was so very sad when Les passed away. He was seeing a Russian girl towards the end of his life, and she was a nightmare. Les used to travel around the world with her; she really took up a big part of his life. I reckon she 'stopped' him from seeing me towards the end. I had a big birthday party lined up at Pontlands Park Hotel, Great Baddow, but for the

Cooper Class: Les and I knocking back ice tea on the ski slopes of Val d'isere, 2000

first time ever Les didn't show up to it, which I believe was because of her. That made me really upset.

One day his son found him in a state in the house; he just wasn't right. I went up to the hospital and met Les coming out, and he told me that they'd given him three months to live. Les died within about four weeks of that news. I was devastated; he was my best friend. He's got an excellent tombstone at Southend, with the 19th hole carved upon it. Les was ever so generous there: he kitted the golf club out with carpets, and he really supported the club. I took up golf because of him.

He was one of the most important people in my life and a big influence on me.

Another wonderful influence on my life was Fluff. I used to work with him, and one day he invited me around his home for dinner. After that, I regularly visited Fluff and his wife Pru for Sunday lunch for about 20 years. Pru worked for me in the carpet shop, and since Fluff's death over 21 years ago, Pru has become such an amazing part of my life. The most important thing about friendship is not arguing. Les, Roy, Fluff, Peter and I never argued. Once you start arguing, that's it. We never had any problems.

HE CROSSED THE CHANNEL IN THIS

Surely one of the most unusual craft ever to have crossed the Channel.

CHELMSFORD carpet store owner Tony Appleton had a double purpose in view when he set out to cross the channel in a 'powered' four-poster bed. This was to launch a new shop in the town's shopping precinct which is to specialise in the sale of beds and to raise funds for the Chelmsford amateur boxing club. He is club president.

Although he overbalanced and fell in the River Chelmer when demonstrating the stability of the craft, the actual crossing from Dover to Calais was completed without mishap.

The four-poster was constructed on a catamaran style hull filled with liquid polystyrene.

Although we were prepared to cover the bed during the crossing this was not required. We did however insure its £300, 40 mph outboard motor.

5. GREAT ADVENTURES

FOUR-POSTER YACHT

I've always been a promotions man. I always come up with ideas on how to promote businesses and people. When I set up my bedding shop I came up with the idea to sail across the English Channel on a powered four-poster bed. A friend of mine built the bed, and we filled the base of it with liquid polystyrene. We did a test on the River Chelmer, which was successful, so I decided to give it a go sailing it from Dover to Calais. I painted the words 'Tony Appleton's Bedding Shop' along the side so the world could see it.

I paid £50 to Captain Hutchins to be escorted across; it was the only legal way to do it. He said yes, probably thinking it was the quickest £50 of his life, believing we would not make it five minutes into the journey, but I proved him wrong. Luck was on our side that day: all the ferries were on strike,

Chelmsford Weekly News coverage of my epic Chelmer Lady channel crossing, 1986

meaning we came into very little traffic. The waves were strong and I had a bottle of rum to keep the cold out. I feared after a few sips I would fall off, never to be seen again, but my time in the Royal Navy gave me good sea legs.

By the time we got over to Calais, I was half cut from the rum. We made it across in only five and a half hours, and a busload of people drove over to Calais so they could cheer us on when we arrived. People could see the boat coming out of the mist and they said it was like mad dogs and Englishmen coming out of the midday sun. We had photographers who came with us, and we made it into the local and national papers. Anybody who goes to Calais today can go to the museum there, where you can see pictures and accounts of everyone including myself who have sailed across in different ways. I was the first and only man to ever sail across on a four-poster bed – I always dare to be different.

ROLLING UP THE CARPET SHOPS

I had the five shops for 18 years, but then things started to go downhill. The businesses began to lose more and more money, and in the end we were actually losing up to £500 a week. Les and I noticed that people from Brentwood were starting to shop in Romford instead. Les and I nearly fell out when he told me to sell my bungalow. I decided not to, it would have been too defeatist. I had to start from scratch again, and sold the business leases. I already had another little shop in Brentwood arcade, which sold remnants and bits like that. That worked out well, but I've always enjoyed doing sales in the evening, working till 8pm every night. I missed being a salesman, knocking on people's doors and making the big cash, so I decided to get back into that.

Money was good and I did that for years, but I hated not having a workplace to go to and missed a routine. I didn't want to lose the momentum. I only gave up selling carpets recently, but I loved that work. Every morning, I used to get dressed for work and go and chat with stall-holders like the late, great showman Swalley Howells, bless him, which set me up for a good day's work.

WHO'S A PRETTY BOY?

When Mum was alive, we used to have a green amazon parrot named Fred, who lived to the grand old age of 50! He used to sit on top of the cage at my mother's house, and one day he flew up to the top of the oak tree, and we had to get scaffold poles to get him down. He used to speak just like my mother, because he would imitate her. When my mother died, we used to have him in my care home, but it was eerie. He used to sound like Mum even after she died. 'Hello Freddd! Hello darling!' he would say when people came into the room.

I didn't realize my lovely Mum had severe problems just before she passed away. We only discovered that she had dementia when she rang Chelmsford Police. We had to get the

Fire Brigade to get into her bedroom door because she had locked herself in. Later on, I was in the carpet shop with Pru when the Police came in to arrest me for trying to poison my mother. Her dementia had driven her to think I was trying to kill her.

The Police understood, but we only realized how serious her situation was at that point. In the first home we sent her to Mum told me she thought the nuns were 'drugging her' to keep her quiet at night. So we moved her to another home at Rettendon. Aunty Flo lived there with her and kept her company, but one day the care home rang me up and told me that my mother had gone missing. It turned out that she had hitch-hiked with some stranger, who had picked her up in the car and dropped her off miles down the road where she had requested to be taken.

We got Mum back and we moved her to a home in Maldon and she was there for the rest of her life. All through my life, Mum and I were very close. We had our ups and downs, but I looked after her right up until she died. She loved it at Maldon Care Home, and it was to be her final home. Mum died in a flutter from a heart attack at the age of 92, just like that.

THE GREAT ATLANTIC AIR RACE

In 1969, the Daily Mail organised a huge competition called the Great Atlantic Air Race. The race was to go from London to New York City, and the fastest competitor to travel the distance would win £6,000, which was a huge amount of money at that time. I thought I would give it a go – why not? I was fit, ready and able, and wanted the winnings and the fame. I had a few connections in America, including a contact in the Hell's Angels Motorbike Club. I made a few phone calls and, after a day or two, I was ready to go.

The race began at the GPO Tower in London. We all took the lift to the top where we had our photos taken by journalists and were briefed. As soon as the whistle went, we chased down the stairs and elevators to get to the ground level. I had a motorbike waiting for me outside on which I raced along to get to Heathrow airport as quickly as possible.

From there, I flew to Shannon airport, and just about made the connection for the next flight to JFK Airport in New York City. Every one of the competitors chose different modes to get to New York. One guy went by RAF Harrier Jump Jet. On arriving into JFK, I was met by a convoy of Hell's Angels. I quickly jumped on the back of one of their motorbikes, and off we sped.

The club had arranged for a fire engine to drive in front of us, with sirens blaring through the streets. The cops tried to stop us, but gave up when they realized they were the Hell's Angels – they didn't stop for anybody! I was wetting myself with how fast we were riding. After what seemed to be the quickest journey from an airport in my life, we arrived at the Empire State Building. All I had to do was get to the top. I ran inside and pushed the button on the lift, but to my horror saw that I had to wait three minutes for it to come down.

A famous journalist and broadcaster, who will remain nameless, was also taking part in the race, and when he saw us coming, he raced to the top and held the lifts up there so we would have to wait even longer. He wanted to mess up our times, cheeky git. The dirty rat didn't end up winning thankfully, but it was still cruel that he did that to the rest of us. After waiting for what felt like a decade for the lift, I finally made it up to the top in eight hours and 22 minutes.

The Hell's Angels found out that I had been beaten to the top and, as you can imagine, they were not very happy with me. I invited them up to the cocktail party we had at the top of the Empire State Building, and bought them all a huge round. Of course, they chose the most expensive drinks. I knew all along that they only wanted to help me so they could take a share in the prize money. I felt bad, but it was a risk we all took to win the money.

I knew before I left that my father was on his deathbed in hospital, so after the race and a couple of cocktails, I had to get straight back to Chelmsford. I rushed up to the Jump Jet winners of the race and asked if I could cadge a lift back with them. The RAF pilot was almost convinced. I said I could lie in between the aisle of the two seats – I was that desperate. But in the end the answer was NO, so I rushed back to JFK and got the next available flight to London.

When I landed I got a train to Chelmsford and met my good friend Frank Eagle, who came with me to the hospital to see my father. Dad had been a heavy smoker his whole life, and he died of lung cancer just after I arrived at the hospital to see him. He was 72.

HIGHER THAN A KITE

A life goal of mine was to learn how to fly. It turned out to be the toughest challenge of my life, but it was worth it in the end. I earned my pilot's license and held it for three years, frequently flying from Southend to Le Touquet. One time I took three friends on board with me, and we went over the English Channel. After a short time, we got into clouds. I knew I wasn't allowed to fly in clouds, so I had to quickly dive down to get out of it.

One guy in the back, turning a bit green from the flying, shouted that he wanted to get out. I asked him how he thought he was going to get out of the plane while we were flying over the Channel. He soon calmed down, and we had lunch at Le Touquet. I got in a panic when I lost the airplane keys; I couldn't find them anywhere. This trip was not going as smoothly as I thought it would. The aero mechanics wired it up to go back to Southend for us, but one of the guys said he was going to travel in another plane home. He never flew with me again!

They dubbed me 'Chelmsford's Superman' when I flew over Selsey Bill, 1986

On another flying adventure I took my niece and her friend, and we flew to Portsmouth for a wedding. When we came back to the airfield the girls started playing hide-and-seek around the blessed airfield while I prepared the plane to leave. I knew that I hadn't got a license to fly at night, and it was getting dark. I started to feel panicked. After a long search, I found them in the nick of time, and we got back to Southend just before nightfall.

The scariest flying experience of all was when I decided to go on a map reading excursion. I got completely and utterly lost. I was on my own and struggled with the map! I looked below me and saw the Thames, and then to my horror, I saw the GPO Tower. I flew around the Tower, which at the time was a £4,000 fine. I watched people eating their lunch through the windows and saw them waving to me. I thought, I better get out of here before I get into trouble!

Because I was so under the radar – quite literally – I didn't get the fine. When I got back to the Southend area, I could see they had sent planes out looking for me, and that's how I found my way back. I have kept that quiet, until now! Gaining that license was the most rewarding challenge I had ever risen

Newholme began life as a hotel when purchased in 1980

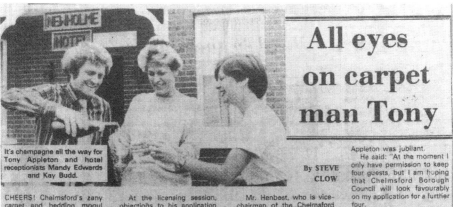

It's champagne all the way for Tony Appleton and hotel receptionists Mandy Edwards and Kay Budd.

All eyes on carpet man Tony

By STEVE CLOW

CHEERS! Chelmsford's zany carpet and bedding mogul Tony Appleton pops champagne to celebrate his new venture into the hotel world.

Tony, well-known for jumping off piers on home-made wings and crossing the Channel on a bed, has got the green light to expand his bed-and breakfast guest house in Great Baddow.

He was granted permission by the town's magistrates to run a bar and restaurant at Newholme Hotel, Baddow Road, which he bought on the spur of the moment while walking his dogs in January.

At the licensing session, objections to his application for a residential and restaurant licence were heard from local publicans and Great Baddow Parish Council.

Mr. Allan Henbest, licensee of the nearby Carpenter's Arms, said he feared that if Mr. Appleton found that his bar was not "paying" he may be tempted to encourage friends to come round and end up running a public house.

He was asked by Mr. Vernon Frost, appearing for Mr. Appleton, "Do you fear that the applicant won't play the game?"

Mr. Henbest, who is vice-chairman of the Chelmsford Licensed Victuallers Association replied: "Yes, this is the danger."

Mrs. Mary Bradford, clerk to the parish council, said she had been instructed to object on the grounds that neighbours were against the scheme.

No neighbours appeared at the hearing, but in granting the licences he was told by the magistrates that "all eyes" were on him to keep the limits set which only allowed the bar to be used by bona fide guests.

After the hearing, Mr.

Appleton was jubilant.

He said: "At the moment I only have permission to keep four guests, but I am hoping that Chelmsford Borough Council will look favourably on my application for a further four.

"Now I am able to run a bar and also offer an evening meal as well as the current bed and breakfast.

"It's always been my ambition to run this type of hotel and when I saw the For Sale notice go up outside the building earlier in the year I immediately decided it would be ideal."

Chelmsford's wealthy bachelor currently lives in a tiny bedroom behind the reception desk at the hotel.

"Let's face it, I own every room in the hotel so I regard it as mine!" he commented.

to, but after three years I decided it was probably safest for everyone if I stayed with feet firmly on the ground.

For 12 years I entered the annual Birdman Competition, jumping off the Selsey Pier. I was dubbed Chelmsford's Superman. I was always in the national papers or in the local news for that. I was attempting to be first man on earth to fly on my own steam. If successful, I would win a £5,000 reward. I didn't have much luck while practicing on Selsey, and had a few crashes. I then practiced on a crane and the rope broke. During a 'dry run' at Southend Pier I armed myself with a crash helmet and life jacket and launched myself into the air. I managed 60 yards before I flopped into the sea.

HOME SWEET NEWHOLME

Newholme House, my care home, sits in the village of Great Baddow near my home. I bought it as a hotel in 1980. At the time, I was dating a woman from Southend called Judy Innel. She owned four care homes, and advised me to turn the hotel into a care home. The reason being that the residents don't go home at the end of the weekend like guests do at a hotel. So, I started off with 10 residents, then 12, then 14, and today there's room for 18. It was all down to Judy, who sadly passed away some time later, that I came to owning and running a care home.

A few years ago, I got asked to do a Toastmaster job in Las Vegas. While I was away, someone called up my care home

Newholme House, today a caring home from home for up to eighteen guests

manager Carmel Walsh to complain that we had too many residents living there. Social Services turned up and looked all over the house, even asking to look in the cellar to see if we had hidden residents secretly down there! They soon saw that we had ample space for the residents, and that we didn't have more people than we should have done, so they left us alone. Carmel dealt with that situation well, and she has been such a wonderful manager and good friend to me during the 26 years she has so far managed Newholme.

The only thing I would change about the care home is the blessed road that lies in front of it. There is a 30mph speed limit along it, and it drives me mad that nobody sticks to it. A few years back, I once parked my car outside the care home. I was only going in for a minute, so I knew I had to be quick. As I stepped out of the car, a pensioner's vehicle went ploughing into the back of my car. I had literally only just stepped away from the car, and I was incredibly lucky to be alive.

Five police cars turned up on the scene within minutes, along with two fire engines. Paramedics told me that if I had still been in the car I would have had terrible whiplash, or much worse. The other car was so smashed up that the pensioner driving it had to be admitted to hospital after being cut from it by firefighters. In more recent years, I have protested by the road with a sign that I made, demonstrating that people should stick to the speed limit.

Someone asked me recently if I would ever sell up my care home, but I truly feel that even if I came into some serious money, I could never abandon it. I love it; it's my stability, and it's a rewarding job. I love to make people happy, and I love talking to the residents to make sure they are well looked after in their sunset years. I would never leave Great Baddow. The bungalow I live in today has been my home for the past 50 years. You would have to carry me out of my home in a box to get rid of me. However much I have travelled abroad, I will never leave this village.

THE CHICKEN RUN

I used to love skiing; it was a great passion of mine. I gave it up only a few years ago. Friends and I would go to destinations like Lake Tahoe and San Moritz. A big group of us would go, including my dear friends Les Cooper, Robert Bartella and Lou Manzi. At the beginning, they put me in ski school until they were confident enough to let me go down the tricky black runs with them. Those were some of the best times of my life. I remember we used to sneak whisky on the slopes

Ice cool in Courchevel, 1980. From left to right: Mike Hardy, Gordon Shields, his brother Stephen Shields, Les Cooper and myself

with us, to keep us warm on the snow. Together we travelled to Courchevel, Switzerland, Austria, Lake Tahoe, and Colorado. Each year was a different place.

I would dress up as a chicken and zoom down the mountain, flapping my arms about. I was always the entertainer; I just loved to make people laugh. I bought a karaoke machine and took it everywhere we went. There were no jukeboxes in the bars up in the mountains, so I would pull out my machine and loved to get everyone singing over their jugs of beer. I sometimes even used to play it while skiing down the mountain.

Eddie the Eagle's instructors take a photo call, 1982. From left to right: Robert Bartella, Gordon Shields, Lou Manzi and yours truly

I had so much fun with my karaoke blizzard buddy Lou Manzi on the slopes. Before we reached the top, Lou and I would start singing karaoke from the lifts, and behind us the Essex boys would join in. The hills were alive with the sound of Elvis impersonators, belting out 'It's Now Or Never' and 'The Wonder Of You'.

Robert Bartella was once up the top of a mountain. He wasn't the best skier, bless his heart. He was with a ski instructor, and as he went down the slope, he fell and rolled all the way down. When he finally reached the bottom, the on-site doctors told him he had broken his arm. That put a dampener on that trip.

I was very fortunate that, with the amount of times we went skiing, I only had one accident, which didn't turn out to be that serious but has affected me for life. It was the fault of another person in our group, who wasn't a confident skier. I watched as he came pounding down the mountain. As he lost control of his skis, he fell and tumbled towards me. I couldn't get out of the way quick enough, and as he came bounding into me, he pushed me over and ran over my head with his ski.

Ever since then, I have had tinnitus – a ringing sound in my ear. There's no cure for it. I have gone to the doctors on countless occasions to work out how to fix it. The problem comes from not having proper ear protection during my time in the Royal Navy, and also this ski accident.

One of our friends moved to Switzerland, and so we decided to do a ski trip there to visit him. He liked a girl who worked in the bar there, and I always like to play tricks and jokes on people. I took a gadget with me that I had bought at the airport. It had an invisible string for holding, and you could attach things to the other end of it. At the push of a button, it would pull whatever item you had attached back to you.

The girl who my friend liked fell for my trick, but it backfired on me! I attached a huge Swiss note to the end of the string, and waited for her to come along and spot it. She bent down to pick it up and as she did, I pressed the button. The note came flying back over to me. I can still see the look on her face when she saw it disappear out of her hand. She came storming up to me, and slapped me right around the face. That wasn't the first or the last time I was slapped around the face!

FITNESS FIRST

About 40 years ago, I read an article on how to live a long and healthy life. It suggested that you should exercise daily, so I bought an exercise bike and I have been training on it for 30 minutes, five days per week, ever since. I also do 100 sit-ups five mornings a week, and 80 lengths of pool every single day. It's such a lovely stretch, and it makes me well, physically and mentally.

When I'm done, I feel like I'm set for the day. Every morning I line up outside the door of the swimming pool, ready to plunge in. I just love it. Even on holiday I keep up the exercise, and then I feel like I can indulge in whatever I please. It keeps me young, and helps me relax. I'm always on the move, but I do this every day, and I find that it really helps me to focus.

CLOSE CALL

One time, on holiday in Tobago with my partner Pru, I decided to go on an early morning swim in the sea. I would often do that, but on this one particular holiday, the sea was really rough. I shouldn't have gone in when there was not another soul around, but I did anyway. It is such a wonderful feeling having the sea all to yourself with no one around on the beach.

But on this particular day, the sea punished me for it. A massive wave came and lifted me up, and it threw me out of the sea, dropping me on the beach. I was knocked out and, once again, lucky to be alive. When I came round, I was still the only person in sight. I had such a headache, and I had to walk back to the hotel and explain what had happened.

After enjoying a delicious breakfast of eggs at the hotel we got on the bus to the airport. When we got to the airport, I began to feel pretty ill, but I got on the plane anyway. Pru told me I must have been bus sick, but I knew it wasn't that. I had been a bus conductor for months and had never got bus sick! It was lucky the sickness didn't come on until we were in the air or they would never have let me on the flight. When we got home, I went straight to Chelmsford hospital and was hospitalised for four days with salmonella poisoning.

6. SHOOTING STARS

WHO'S THAT WITH TONY APPLETON?

For many years I have had my summer holidays in Majorca. One night, while I was sitting in a bar I got talking to this blonde bombshell. A flashbulb went off from a camera, and the photo was printed a week later in a popular Swedish magazine. It turned out that I was chatting away to the well-known movie star Anita Ekberg, famous for starring in the film *La Dolce Vita*. The paparazzi dubbed me as her jet-set lover from Chelmsford, and the picture was soon all over the media. All I did was sit next to her and chat to her, but soon enough, I was getting fan mail!

After that, things went a little quiet on the publicity front until I teamed up with *Essex Chronicle* photo-journalist Steve 'Scoop' Clow. We used to do military-style operations, meticulously planning how to get into VIP tents and events and how to get pictures with the jet set. My friends thought I

was mad, but it's all about the buzz. The adrenaline buzz you get waiting to snap a photo – you can't beat it.

I first met Steve when he was a taxi driver of all things. Journalists were on strike across the country, but he refused to stand on the picket line outside his paper, and took up driving over Christmas to feed his wife and three kids. The third time he dropped me off outside my Market Road carpet shop, I invited him in to look at all my celebrity photos on the walls and he was impressed.

Steve suggested teaming up 'professionally' as my stunt co-ordinator, and he has since become a good friend. He's a great gate-crashing colleague; he always comes up with game plans with a 99 per cent success rate and we get on such a high with it all.

Our best hits have been at the Bob Hope Classic Pro-Am golf tournaments where we would snap loads of Hollywood stars like Victor Mature, Ernest Borgnine, James Garner, Telly Savalas – the A list is endless – as well as British stars such as Bruce Forsythe, Sean Connery and Eric Sykes. I even dodged armed secret service bodyguards to pose with US President Gerald Ford.

A helicopter flew in Joan Collins who was dating a guy the media dubbed 'Bungalow Bill' I thought that with my bungalow and swimming pool I could be next in line. Steve

Melting the Iceberg: Anita with her 'Jet Set lover from Chelmsford',
the carpet bagger!

raced off to Jessops after he took snaps of the two of us. He was back in no time and I showed them to Joan who was impressed. She autographed them, but that was all!

Once I was invited to take part in a live broadcast from Moor Park to the BBC studios of *The Six O'Clock Show* hosted by Michael Aspel, but at the last minute the producer pulled the plug on me appearing. Steve came up with a plan. Just as the interviewer went live, I walked up to his mic and announced: "Can I have my photograph with you, Michael?" I heard Aspel gasp: "Oh, No! It's that man again, Tony

I rolled out the red carpet for Dynasty star Dame Joan Collins at the

Bob Hope Classic, Moor Park

Appleton!" and promptly invited me to be his star guest on the next show!

FLASHBULB APPLETON

After snatching hundreds upon hundreds of photos and gate-crashing celebrity parties, I was nicknamed 'Flashbulb Appleton' by the media. With this encouragement, I decided I wanted to give a really huge superstar the opportunity to have their photo taken with me. Elizabeth Taylor was holding a press

Presenting Dame Elizabeth Taylor with her favourite orchid flower at London Palladium.
Photo: John McLellan, copyright Essex Chronicle.

conference for *Little Foxes*, before her West End stage debut, so I invited along a BBC TV outfit headed by journalist, Janet Street-Porter, who wanted to be in on my next little venture.

Steve managed to wangle official press passes for the event. It was packed with paparazzi, and Janet's clued-up crew were ready for action. When the time was right, Steve nodded and I jumped over the barrier and slipped past her bodyguards. I held out an orchid dyed violet, the colour of her eyes, which I knew was her favourite flower.

Liz was overwhelmed and quipped, "Oh my god, I thought you was the producer!" Her stunned heavies who bundled me back over the barrier all got the sack. I was chucked out of the theatre, but really glad that *Essex Chronicle* snapper John McLellan had taken a great series of pictures and when we saw Janet's footage on the *Six O'Clock Show*, I was back on another month-long high.

ON THE ROPES

On October 17, 1989, for the first time ever, Mohammad Ali and fellow heavyweight champions Joe Frazier and George Foreman appeared together in the UK to launch the video *Champions Forever* at the London Arena. Of course, I was at the press conference waiting in the wings. I was poised ready to get a 'selfie' with three champs in front of the world's press, having already had my picture taken with Ali in Las Vegas 17 years earlier.

Gatecrashing Muhammad Ali and Joe Frazier, 1989

Steve again gave me the nod, and while bodyguards were staring at the TV cameras instead of keeping a watch out for the 'Flashbulb', I leapt over a barrier and walked behind the seated champs. They all posed for me and Frazier smiled as he remarked: "This is one wild guy!" You can watch it on You Tube.

Now let me tell you about my first meeting with Ali in Las Vegas. I managed to blag my way onto the boxing ring at Caesar's Palace before his big fight with Joe Bugner. Henry Cooper was in the ring with me and I told him I was going to get a picture with Ali, but he shook his head: "No chance."

Lady Margaret Thatcher accepts my carnation birthday present for hubby Dennis and presented it to him on the platform, Brighton Conference, 1983

I then got into Ali's dressing room by pretending to be a reporter, but his heavies told me to go away.

Ali heard the racket and said, "Leave him alone." He then told me to meet him in the carpark in 15 minutes. When we met up Ali handed me his boxing shorts, which I auctioned off for charity at Chelmsford Boys Boxing Club when I was its president. As for the photo of him and me, well it never came out because it was so dark in the carpark and the flashbulb never went off. I did get The Greatest's shorts at least – proof of yet another successful gate-crash.

FAMOUS FACES

Another famous politician snap was when I managed to get my picture with then-Prime Minister Margaret Thatcher. It was one of the more tricky shots to get, as it was at the heavily policed 1984 Brighton Conservative conference. She had a lot of security guards around her, and they could see I was hanging around for a picture.

The Police asked me what I was there for, and I told them I wanted a picture taken with her. The Police warned me that I might get shot if I approached her. I politely then asked the security guards if they would ask her to come out, and happily, she did. I got the photo! On TV she used to come across as tough, but she was very friendly and warm towards me.

According to Sir Terry I am "the most unwelcome guest" but he made me feel right at home on his Wogan Show!

Who are those Rolling Stones with Tony Appleton?

One of the not-so-nice responses to my photograph collecting was when I came face-to-face with American actress Raquel Welch at her book signing. I waited in the queue, and when I got to the front I jumped behind her to get a picture. She quickly responded by slapping me round the face.

I learned that you must never ask celebs if they minded having a picture with you – just do it. Ninety-nine per cent of the time they are happy to pose, if only to 'get him out of the way.' It was a hobby that I just couldn't control. There was no end – where do you stop? I did wonder whether they might have wanted to be seen with me? Were they looking out for me

Rocking and raising money with Suzi Quattro at an Elvis dance

at a premiere or a book signing so they could be photographed with me? Had I become equally the celebrity?

Over time I have collected over 2,000 photographs with the rich and famous. Even today, I am the most photographed person with celebrities in this country – if not the world – so I decided to hold an exhibition at the Shire Hall in Chelmsford. Steve helped put together the *Shooting the Stars* show, as he had taken many of the shots himself. It was held to raise money for charity to support disabled children.

After the exhibition, I was interviewed on prime-time television and did my rounds of the studios. I appeared on

My favourite dogs Giant Schnauzer Claude (left) and Doberman Pinscher Daniel

Terry Wogan's Friday night live show, and I was even invited to Monica Lewinsky's book launch here in the UK. Michael Aspel interviewed me on his show several times, calling me, "That man Appleton again!" At the time I had five carpet shops, so I found that it was something fun to do as a hobby outside work. I spent thousands of pounds traveling around the world to get pictures of celebrities. Terry Wogan predicted that soon people would start asking "Who's that star with Tony Appleton?" rather than the other way round!

MY FAMILY AND OTHER ANIMALS

My beloved cat Sam slept on my bed every night of his life till he was 20 years of age. He was the oldest cat in Great Baddow, and it did me in when he died earlier this year. I used to jog five miles a day with my Doberman, Daniel. He was such a lovely dog. I also was given an expensive Bengal Tiger Cat. My friends bought it for me for my 50th birthday. It was a real beast. He didn't last long; he went out hunting every night and got hit by a car.

They are wild cats, and you have to keep them in a cage, something that I did not like to do. Of course there was also Fred, the parrot who imitated Mum and entertained my care home guests. There was a pet pig named Tony, and a giant Schnauzer called Claude. I had a second giant, Douglas, who everyone called Douglas the Delinquent. One of my residents had a wooden leg in the home and the Delinquent ran up the road with it in his mouth. What a palaver!

THE RINGING AND SINGING PARTY

I twice stood as an independent candidate to choose the next Brentwood MP. One of those times I stood along with another independent, broadcaster Martin Bell. Martin and I got along really well, and we really got each other's sense of humour. When a lady asked me, "What are you going to do about parking in this town if you get in?" I replied, "I'm the Ringing and Singing Party. When I'm in the House of Commons, I'll wake them up with my bell when they've all fallen asleep!" She gave me a look, which told me I was mad, and then she walked off.

The first year I got 50 votes, and the next year I tripled it and got 152 votes. A lot of people in the area took it seriously, as you can imagine. But we also had some supporters who just understood our humour, and voted for us for a laugh. Looking back on it now, I would have been in real trouble if I had actually got elected.

In recent years, you may have seen me in Chelmsford city centre walking up and down with a sign protesting in support of its PCSOs whose jobs were under threat due to the slashing of Essex Police budgets. I just couldn't stand to see good people put out of decent jobs. In the end, the top brass decided to let them stay in the High Street following widespread anger.

LADIES AND GENTLEMEN, IT'S TONY APPLETON!

Nearly 30 years ago, my good friend Robert Bartella told me that I would make a fantastic Toastmaster. Robert owns Pontlands Park Hotel, Great Baddow, and so had seen many Toastmasters over the years. I listened to Robert's advice, and did my research to find the best Toastmaster tutor in the world to train me up. Having completed 1,000 Royal functions, I found that Royal Toastmaster Ivor Spencer was the best, so I got in contact with him to arrange an interview.

During the interview, Ivor asked me about my many jobs, so I listed off each one of them. For some unknown reason, I failed. I think that I was the only person at that stage to have failed the entrance exam. I returned the following March and passed with flying colours, so I accompanied Ivor Spencer for a year, mirroring his work, learning from a masterful master of ceremonies.

As Toastmaster, you have to always be smart and on time, which is perfect for me having been trained in the Navy! For every job I do as a Toastmaster, I am always there two hours early. Today, there are far too many Toastmasters working all across the country. The cake is only so big, so my assignments have lessened. But over the years, I've had some special gigs.

LOST VEGAS

On one occasion I was in my office in the garden of my care home – the shed, as everyone calls it – when we had a phone call come through to the main house. Gill my bookkeeper connected us, and she told me that it was America on the phone. They said that they were looking for a Toastmaster to go to Las Vegas, to help with a TGIFriday's launch. Thankfully they didn't know they were talking to a man in a shed, and I got the job.

They flew Pru and I out to Vegas, and I worked for two days, then Pru and I drove to Scottsdale, Arizona for a break. I decided to bring a British Sat Nav along with us, and we set off for Scottsdale. One hour later we ended up back in bloody Vegas again – we had gone round in a circle! Eventually, after six hours, we arrived in Scottsdale. A friend of ours had told us that we would love the heat of the desert, but when we arrived, we were surprised to see that it was chucking it down with rain. It hadn't rained for 18 months, but it rained for five days straight for us.

Having enough of that, we drove to Palm Springs. The first night we stayed on a Native American reservation, which was probably the worst place I had ever stayed in my entire life. The next day, we moved to another hotel. I got so fed up with driving out there that we abandoned the car at the hotel and got a taxi from Palm Springs to Los Angeles Airport. That assignment was the highlight of my Toastmastering career.

I gained a lot of experience over the years, and I am so very proud that the Royal Blackheath Golf Club, the oldest golf club in the UK, asked me to become their resident Toastmaster.

BRIDEZILLA

A good Toastmaster makes a wedding or event flow. At one particular wedding, the bride turned up in her beautiful white dress, but stood too close to the exhaust of a nearby car, burning the back of her dress. She was furious.

Later at the reception, when I introduced the Bride and Groom, I pronounced the bride's name wrong. She came pounding up and screamed at me. She was adamant that I had got it wrong, so quick as a flash I had an idea to save my bacon. I went up to the videographer when nobody was around, and we did a reshoot. In the video I said her name correctly. I got away with that one, thank goodness, but you have to think on your feet.

The thing with Town Crying and Toastmastering is you can go on for too long a time in your later years. A lot of people take it too far; they don't know when to pack it up. Even the late, great Ivor Spencer didn't know when to stop. At the end of his career, he made some big mistakes. He wasn't what he used to be, and it was difficult for me to watch that happening to a man I very much admire. When it comes to that point in your life, you just need to know when to hang up the gavel, or bell. As the song goes, you got to know when to fold 'em and when to walk away.

7. LORD OF GREAT BADDOW AND ROYAL TOWN CRIER

OYEZ! OYEZ! OYEZ!

In 1993, on the advice of Robert Bartella, I bought the title 'Lord of Great Baddow'. I have the proper deeds for it, and I like to call myself Lord Anthony Appleton, although when hotels find out my title they often try to charge me more! As the Manorial Lord I am allowed to have a market stall in the village three times a year, and it's all a bit of fun, plus mineral extraction rights – but I am not about to hire a JCB and go digging for gold!

One year, I held a fundraising fete in the village to raise money for charity, and I dressed up as Lord of the Manor of Great Baddow. A child told me that I looked like a Town Crier in my outfit. That evening, by coincidence, the phone rang that was to change my life. The person on the other end said, "Tony, I know you're a Master of Ceremonies, but you don't know a Town Crier do you? I need one!" I said, "Yeah, you're talking to one." So I decided there and then that I was a Town Crier. I trained in the mirror, shouting from my diaphragm for six hours without losing my voice. I plastered the town with leaflets. And thus, I became Tony Town Crier.

Now I can say with confidence, if you don't believe I am a Town Crier, Google me – I'm only the most famous Town Crier there is. When a woman asked me recently about this, I replied, "Sweetheart, I'm Tony Appleton, I'm everywhere." That's what comes with fame. A few criers are professionally jealous of my success and notoriety. I have done the hard graft

Lord of the Manor of Great Baddow

of years of training to become the world's most well-known Town Crier; it wasn't on a plate.

THAT RINGS A BELL

Up until the 19th century, literacy was low amongst the majority of the population, but as long as there has been news to share, there has been a messenger to deliver it. The Town Crier can be traced back to 1066 AD, after the Battle of Agincourt, when news of Britain's invasion by William the Conqueror was passed from town to town by individuals specifically employed to call out the king's proclamations. Proclamations, laws, and news may well have been written on paper, but the Town Crier usually passed them to the general public: the first talking newspaper.

'Oyez! Oyez! Oyez!' – roughly translated as 'hark!' or 'listen!' – became a familiar call in town squares, markets and public meeting places all over Great Britain. It was a summons to townspeople, to gather to listen to news about plagues, victories, far off lands, royal births, executions and more. The Town Crier would announce it reading from a paper, and then nail it to the door of the local inn. The result of this tradition has been the making of the newspaper, the post, the post office, and in more recent times, posting messages on the Internet. Along with this fascinating history, another thing I have learned from being a Town Crier is that when you're in front of the world's press, you can't make a mistake.

BOXING CLEVER

Before the 2008 recession, I had so many crying jobs that I couldn't cope with the workload, so I trained up Steve Clow and his journalist colleague Peter Baker. We called ourselves The Three Criers – Voice of the Nation. We enjoyed lots of assignments for a whole variety of companies, the best employer being Box Clever. We cried individually at their TV rental shops all over the UK. We only cry together at important Royal events, celebrating anniversaries and birthdays.

The Three Criers proclaiming Her Majesty The Queen's 90th birthday at Windsor Palace

In my view, the Royal Family is the backbone of our country. The tourism and money it brings to our wonderful country is significant, and we would be in serious trouble without them. We live in a world where there is so much dreadful news, but the Royals always give us so much pleasure. I believe some other nations might even be envious of the United Kingdom for its democratic Monarchy, as it is such a special thing.

Alongside my title of Romford, Great Baddow and Bury St Edmunds' Town Crier, I also am known as the Royalist Town Crier. I announced and proclaimed the marriage of HRH Prince William and Kate Middleton on April 29, 2011, at Westminster Abbey. We Three Criers stood outside Buck House dressed in our bright red matching uniforms made by Royal tailor Geoffrey Golding.

We cheered the crowd on, singing songs and chanting, and I took the lead role to spread the huge buzz that was building up around the event. (We had the foresight to take along stepladders so that we would be seen and, more importantly, heard amongst the huge throng on that big day.)

In 2012, I took part in the colourful closing ceremony of the London Olympics and received a letter from David Cameron, thanking me for my hard work as a volunteer.

Standing Out in a Crowd at Prince William and Princess Kate's Wedding

HRH PRINCE GEORGE

In July 2013 I announced the arrival of the Duke and Duchess of Cambridge's son, HRH Prince George, directly outside the Lindo wing of St Mary's Hospital, London. I became a national icon for the birth when TV cameras broadcast my proclamation to millions live across the globe.

As part of my meticulous preparation I asked my good friend, Tom Corby MVO – a title given to him personally by Her Majesty The Queen – to compose a suitable proclamation for my scroll. Tom, who writes Royal books, is a former Royal Correspondent with the Press Association and knows the protocol.

Timing was essential to the operation. Well before the birth of Prince George, I knew the element of surprise was going to make my mission a success, so we purposefully kept away from the maternity wing until the last minute.

Steve and I came up with the game plan. As soon as we got a 'deep throat' tip off that a Prince had been born, we dashed out of our nearby hotel and jumped into a taxi, all dressed for the occasion. "Taxi!" I yelled. "Take me to the door of St Mary's Hospital, right away." Without looking up, the cabbie said, "Right, sir. Right away, sir," as if he was talking to someone from the Palace.

Proclaiming Princess Charlotte's birth, outside St Mary's Hospital,
London, 2013

Although the road was cordoned off, they still allowed taxis through. I got out of the cab, unrolled my scroll and made the first proclamation. Steve told me to be bold as brass, to walk straight past the two duty Police Officers, as if I had been sent by the Palace. I announced Prince George's birth from the pavement, then the media begged me go up the steps and make the proclamation again, and the Police let me. The world's press all wanted to interview me. I had camera flashes coming from every angle, and mics shoved into my face, wanting to know all about the 'Royal Crier'.

This was the biggest gate-crash we had ever pulled off. I couldn't believe it. The next day, I woke up and it was all over the world media. The American broadcasters claimed I was a fake and a phony, but I'm not; I really am a professional Town Crier. Criers have been around for centuries, announcing births, executions and weddings. That's what the Town Crier has always done. I had put what had become a somewhat eccentric hobby for the elderly on the front page and on every news bulletin across the world.

My patriotic proclamation was world famous in no time, promoting the time-honoured role of Town Criers. There were a lot of eyes on me that day. I'm colourful, loud, and stand out in the crowd – precisely what a Town Crier needs to be!

It wasn't until after the Cambridges stood on the steps of the Lindo Wing to introduce Prince George to the world that

Oklahomans could almost hear me proclaiming the birth of Prince George!

BIG 12 MEDIA DAYS

From the outside

The perception of OSU football has changed, Gina Mizell writes.

PAGE 10

BENEFIT CONCERT

Ready to rock

The Flaming Lips will co-headline tonight's "Rock for Oklahoma" concert.

PAGE 15A

THE OKLAHOMAN

TUESDAY, JULY 23, 2013   REACHING MORE THAN 475,000 PEOPLE EACH DAY   NEWSOK.COM   OKLAHOMAN.COM
75¢

Veronica case may get 'messy'

BY MICHAEL OVERALL
Tulsa World
michaeloverall@tulsaworld.com

The hearing was kept secret until Monday, but Baby Veronica's biological father went before a Cherokee Nation court last week to have other family members declared joint guardians.

In the middle of a custody battle with her adoptive parents in South Carolina, Dusten Brown had to leave Monday for mandatory Oklahoma National Guard training.

Giving them the power to make legal and medical decisions for Veronica while he's out of state, the Cherokee court granted temporary guardianship to his wife, Robin Brown, and his parents, Tommy and Alice Brown.

The tribal court order came just hours before the state Supreme Court of South Carolina decided last Wednesday to terminate Brown's parental rights and give Veronica back to the adoptive parents.

The timing was coincidental, Cherokee officials said. But the tribe asked the South Carolina court to reconsider its decision.

"It makes a complicated case even more complicated," said Chrissi Nimmo, the tribe's assistant attorney general.

"If they move forward with a final adoption decree, it makes this a very messy, very complicated case."

Nearly 4 years old now, Veronica has lived with her father in Nowata, an hour north of Tulsa, for the past 19 months.

But her adoptive parents in South

SEE CASE, PAGE 2A

HEAR, YE! HEAR, YE! IT'S A BOY!

The arrival of a new royal baby imbued the pomp and pageantry of Buckingham Palace with an extra sense of history Monday as thousands of reporters, Londoners and tourists awaited the most-anticipated birth announcement in years. Outside the hospital where the Duchess of Cambridge gave birth, Tony Appleton, a town crier dressed in traditional robes and an extravagant feathered hat, shouted the news and rang a bell. The baby boy, born at 4:24 p.m. and weighing 8 pounds 6 ounces, will be third in line to the throne behind Prince Charles and Prince William, and is likely to be monarch one day.
Story, Page 3A.

PALÉO:
C'EST PARTI
POUR
SIX JOURS
DE CONCERTS
PAGES 25-28

MARDI 23 JUILLET 2013 · N° 204 · **FR. 2.40**   (TVA 2.5% incluse) · France voisine 1.85 €   www.lematin.ch

**BÉBÉ DE CATHERINE
ET WILLIAM**

C'EST UN
GARÇON!

PAGES 3-5

Another front page proclaiming the birth of Prince George

the media learned I hadn't actually been invited to announce the birth. They suddenly turned on me calling me a fake – the 'liar crier' – even though I never claimed to be the Palace's official Town Crier.

Millions of TV viewers across the world loved seeing my colourful costume and hearing my proclamation outside the

106

Lindo Wing. Before I appeared hundreds of broadcasters were scratching their heads about what more to say. What clinched it was that most of the assembled media did not know about the Royal birth, but thanks to our secret tip-off, I did. THAT was why they all thought I had come from the Palace!

News presenters all over the world had to make their apologies: Ellen from the Ellen show, Rachel Maddow, the Saturday Night Show and numerous other shows were apologizing for jumping to the wrong conclusion, labelling me a complete fraud who dressed up as Town Crier for a laugh.

HRH PRINCESS CHARLOTTE

When the Duke and Duchess of Cambridge announced that they were expecting their second child, I decided to ask them, out of politeness, if I could proclaim the new birth. After writing to them, with the help of Tom Corby, I received a lovely response in which they 'welcomed' my offer, saying they had no objection whatsoever. A Royal seal of approval! I had the letter laminated and hung it around my neck with a red ribbon. I was ready to show any Police Officer or security guard my 'official' invitation. A 'fake' Town Crier no more!

Steve and I realised that this May 2015 proclamation would be a difficult one to pull off because security services and Police would be ready and waiting for me. If they saw me coming, they might stop me at the barriers. We knew the timing had to be perfect. We booked into another London hotel, had a pint at the bar and, just as we were ordering a second, our insider called to tip me off that a princess had been born. We caught a black taxi – just like the first time – and on the way we updated my scroll. It must have taken three minutes from the moment we heard the news to our arrival at the hospital. I climbed up, once again, on to the steps of the Lindo Wing.

This time, the media were waiting for me and the minute I jumped out of the cab, we heard them: "Tony, Tony, look this way!" Two Met Police officers and a plainclothes senior detective recognised me, as hundreds of Fleet Street and international snappers turned their zoom lenses towards me and TV cameras rolled.

I made my first proclamation on the steps of the Lindo Wing, and then was asked to repeat it by many presenters for each country's cameras. I repeated the cry at least 15 times that day, and then had interviews with over a dozen TV crews all uploaded on YouTube.

At both Royal occasions Steve followed me out of the taxi, his iPhone5 set on movie mode, shooting exclusive close-up stuff. Some of the press pack stuck behind the barriers were so fed up they complained out loud to the Police to turf him out, but they ignored them because we are simply the best.

The next day, my proclamation was on the front cover of just about every newspaper and magazine in the world and all over the internet. It made the front cover of OK, and Hello! as well as appearing on BBC Breakfast and CNN, to name but a few. The world's media rightly concluded that because the Police did not intervene, I had been given the Royal seal of approval.

When HRH Prince William and HRH Prince Harry were born, I had only just started my Town Crying career, so I didn't announce their births. I have gotten more professional, you might say, as I go along. After Princess Charlotte's birth, we had phone calls and emails from Town Criers all across the world, thanking me for putting us back on the map. I felt high as a kite from the response. It took us a month to calm down from the whole thing. Weeks later, I was still getting phone calls from the media – live interviews in Tokyo, Skype calls with the Australians, etc. These experiences have given me the opportunity to wave the flag for the Royals who have my deepest respect and admiration.

WAKING UP SUPERMODELS

Soon I was asked to work with beautiful models on a Chinese reality TV show called iSupermodel. It was a very popular show in China, watched by billions in Southeast Asia. For six weeks, they featured me in their TV competition – which girl would win and become the next big thing? They had to do all sorts of things: parachuting, sailing and more.

I drove down to Surrey every day to meet the TV crew at the £6 million house where the girls stayed. Each day, I learned a new script in five minutes, which I had to do first thing at the crack of dawn. I woke them up with the new cry and my town-crying bell. It was so hard to remember my lines, especially when they were in Chinese.

Our best outside location was near Trafalgar Square where the leggy hopefuls took part in an open-air catwalk, but it soon poured down. While everyone took shelter, I decided to cheer us all up. Steve threw me his umbrella and I did a turn with *Singing in the Rain,* earning a round of applause from the Chinese models and film crew. Never one to miss a trick, Steve filmed it all for YouTube!

UPPERS AND DOWNERS

People must have professional training to be a Town Crier. Ivor Spencer, the famous Toastmaster, decided to launch a Town Crying academy. He called me up and said that, in his opinion, I was the best Town Crier in the world and would I like to be headmaster at the academy. It was very flattering! We set up the school in a hotel in Dulwich. Unemployed people, out-of-work actors – all types – all came to the school to learn the tricks of the trade. I taught them how to ring the bell and how to project their voice. We showed our students how to dress as a Town Crier, how to perform and how to deal with pesky kids and grumpy adults.

One long-established Town Crier society got the ache and tried to sue us for setting up the school. They objected to me calling myself the best Town Crier in the world. They told the media they were going to take me to court, but dropped it in the end because it was the personal opinion of Ivor Spencer! We were only doing a good thing, teaching the art of town crying. I only learned about this society when I was on my way to London one day and read about their professional jealousy in the Evening Standard. Anyone can be a Town Crier; you just have to buy a decent uniform. But to be the best, you have to be tutored by the best.

I must admit I was disappointed and hurt when I wrote to Chelmsford Borough Council to offer my services as the official Town Crier for the City and never received a reply. Despite all of my promotional efforts for the City, that old saying rings true: "A prophet has no honour in his own town." So I call myself the Unofficial Chelmsford Town Crier. For years, I was Town Crier of Walthamstow. I used to walk the market four times during the Christmas period, ringing my bell. Happily, I am also adopted and appreciated by Romford Havering, Bury St Edmunds and my lovely village of Great Baddow.

SUITED AND BOOTED

After my double Royal success, it was time to celebrate with a new uniform and get togged up for the Queen's birthday celebrations. I returned to Royal tailor Geoffrey Golding of St Albans, who made the original uniforms for us three Criers. His talented team spent 90 hours making the badges alone,

one of which was to play a vital role in catching the attention of Her Majesty The Queen.

I couldn't believe how heavy the uniform was. It may be the cost of a King's ransom, but you do get your money's worth with the Royal tailor. He gets his share of publicity too, by the way. I noticed a newspaper clipping in his tailor's shop with a photograph of him outside Number 10 Downing Street, tape measure around his neck. It was all about the whistle he was making for Prime Minister David Cameron. Mr Golding really is a celebrity tailor, miles better and a lot cheaper than the London mob. Wearing his gleaming new outfit for six hours is not an easy job, but it's a labour of love, especially the tricorn hat, which is adorned with patriotic red, white and blue ostrich feathers.

Once I was doing a gig on the streets of Chelmsford, and some youths swiped away my hat in broad daylight. Luckily, the Police chased them when I cried out loudly " STOP! Thief!" The £500 hat was returned to me, and the troublemakers had stern words from the Police.

I feel now that I have achieved my goals with town crying. I can't see myself retiring, but I have done so much – what else can I do? As long as I'm healthy, I will do it because I enjoy it so much. I like being a showman: I get dressed up in my uniform, get on the train, and just love it when people come up and ask if they can have their photograph taken with *me*!

THE NAKED CRIER

It's great to be hired for a fun job. I well remember when my second cousin, Gemma Appleton, who was then working as a film editor for Jamie Oliver in London, called me up with the offer of a gig. Jamie was about to have his 40th birthday, and his loyal staff wanted to give him a big surprise. Gemma asked if I wouldn't mind coming along to wish him happy birthday as Town Crier, so of course, I just had to! I got in all my gear, took the train up and met Gemma.

Congratulating Jamie Oliver on his 40th Birthday, 2015

Jamie was pulled into a pretend meeting. Then he was arrested by Star Wars storm troopers who noisily paraded him through the office. Jamie, the storm troopers, and all of the employees came out onto the street in an even bigger parade to his nearby restaurant. I greeted Jamie with a cry, which had him in stitches, especially when I cried that he was conceived at the end of Southend Pier.

Since then I've announced the Diamond Jubilee, the Golden Jubilee and many other glorious occasions. In 2012, Heathrow Airport called me up. They wanted me to welcome Olympic tourists into the country. I danced and rang my bell, proclaiming, "Hey! It's the dancing Town Crier! Welcome to England!"

COOKING UP A STORM

I've made frequent appearances on TV for my photograph collection and for town crying, but one year I decided to try something out of the ordinary. I heard *Britain's Got Talent* were doing auditions and I thought, why not? I went on and sang my favourite Elvis number, *The Wonder of You* – a song I saw Elvis perform himself in 1974. They were sufficiently impressed and put me through to the next stage. I went up there two or three times to audition and eventually I got on TV. BGT judge Piers Morgan told me live that I couldn't sing! "At least I didn't get the sack from the Daily Mirror!" I replied. Piers didn't have a lot to say about that.

After that, I appeared on Simon Cowell's television show, *Food Glorious Food*, hosted by Carol Vorderman. I cooked my grandmother's bread and butter pudding dish, with a dash of Pusser's Traditional Dark Navy Rum. The winner could win £20,000, so of course I was eager to have a shot at it. They later made a cookery book about the show, which I featured in with my recipe. I was filmed at my care home. The TV crew were there for eight hours filming me cooking up the dish. Later on, Carol interviewed me for the show. I didn't quite win, but despite being a runner-up, I was very pleased with the experience.

After each time I appeared on the show, the phone would not stop ringing. I had magazines like *Woman's Own* calling me up to feature the recipe. I was also contacted by a number of big hotels who wanted to have my dish on their menu. It's available at Pontlands Park Hotel, Great Baddow, so make a beeline for a unique Appleton sweet.

THE QUEEN AND I

Meeting Her Majesty The Queen has been a lifelong ambition of mine. In 2016, outside Buckingham Palace, I proudly announced the day she became Britain's longest reigning monarch, the day she overtook her great-great-grandmother, Queen Victoria. It was a fantastic feeling to be involved in such a special occasion. There were a thousand people there, all wanting to congratulate her on her achievement.

NEBUCHADNEZZAR

The Royals have always been important to me. As a member of Ivor Spencer's Guild of Professional Toastmasters, we presented the Queen Mother every birthday with a huge Nebuchadnezzar, equivalent to 20 ordinary champagne bottles, delivered to her London home. Our president Ivor always used to get two Nebs, just in case. One year a bottle fermented in his garage and exploded everywhere! We were so lucky that we hadn't given that bottle to the Queen Mum. When Ivor told the Queen Mother about the explosion, she agreed that it was a good job it went off before the presentation!

Toasting HM The Queen Mother's 96th birthday at Sandringham, 1996

During the Queen Mother's life, I was friendly with William Tallon, nicknamed 'Backstairs Billy' who was her valet. When she passed away he became redundant, sad really, because he was a great character and very loyal.

8. FOREVER YOUNG

For the past 50 years, I have spent my holidays on sunny Majorca. Islander Ricky Lash, a good friend of mine, always gave me advice on what to do for self-promotion. He lived to 100 years of age, and I always felt like he acted so much younger than he was. He loved the sun and keeping healthy, just like I do, but I could never live abroad. I like my routine and being near my care home.

I spend a lot my spare time thinking about getting older. I wake up every day and think to myself, where have the years gone? I hate it when people ask how old I am; I don't like to be reminded. I am grateful to have had a good life, and I am not ready to stop yet. Whether it was my doing or someone else's, just about everything I've done has been documented. Take as many pictures of your life as you can, and put them in albums so you can look back on what you have achieved. I have had such a happy life, and keeping happy is what keeps you young. Being a Town Crier makes people happy, so it makes me happy too. Sometimes I feel like I'm drunk on my own adrenaline.

There are so many people who walk around with a long face, which drives me mad. They think they have the world on their shoulders, but nothing can be that bad. I wake up in the morning, and I enjoy the day fully until I go to bed. I don't cry about the next day, I don't think about the next day. Live for today – that's my motto! I always try to make up if I have a fall out with a good mate. Forgive and forget because life is too short for grudges. It's harder to form relationships as you get older; your old friends are the best ones anyway, so hang onto them.

MISTER GADGET

My passion for gadgets is well known. I was the first karaoke man in Chelmsford. I knew I had to get one when they first came out, for my parties and just for a laugh. I was also the first person with a video cassette player, a mobile phone and a VHS-Compact video camera. Remember those huge mobiles that you held with two hands against the side of your face? Anything that comes out new, I'll have it. I am Mr Gadget man.

Recently, I bought a flashy hover board that you stand on and move around. I practiced on my driveway and had the good sense to wear a crash helmet. They are a nightmare to step off. The last time I went on one I crashed to the floor and was saved by my old Town Crying suit, although I really bashed my elbow. Steve's crazy idea was to go outside Buckingham

Palace and zoom along Town Crying, but that went out the window after that knockback.

GET IT AT GRIPPERS

If you want something, just get it. Get it on finance and live for today, but make certain you can pay it back as you earn. Enjoy yourself. If I hadn't taken a loan to get my Jaguar E-Type, I would never have had it. I paid it back, and all's well.

Over the years, I've had people ask me to go out for a beer with them. They ask me how it is that I have become so successful. I say to them that you have to promote yourself. If you sent a letter today and just wrote Tony Appleton, it would get to me, because everyone knows who I am now. I've made my name; I've pushed my name.

I have people chasing me up the high street telling me they saw me on a TV show, or they saw me do a talk. People ask me how to advertise for their companies, or themselves. The only way to get yourself in the paper is to do something different. That's what you have to do to get noticed: be original, be eye-catching, be bold, and – so long as it's lawful – do not ask permission.

PARTNERS IN CRIME

The one person I am most proud of is Joseph, my Godson. I have been his guardian ever since he was a boy. Usually you have to have a degree to get into what he now does, but there is an old saying that fits – it's not what you know, but who you know. Stewart Blake, from a London firm, another very good friend, agreed to take Joe on when he was about 16. He gave him a chance, so he went to Moorgate in London as a trainee and he's thriving. I call Joe 'the Wolf of Moorgate'. Joe is now able to buy a home, and he's only 25.

I got Joe a VW for his birthday – my that was a big surprise for him. He drove it down the drive when he hadn't passed his test yet. He was so happy. He's a very likeable boy, and he makes good friends. He knows that I look after him. He

Relaxing in Majorca

respects me a lot, and sends me cards every birthday, Father's Day and Christmas. When he was younger, I went to every single one of his parents' evenings. Since then, Joe asks my advice frequently, which makes me so proud.

Robert Bartella, his son Jason, and Lisa his wife, have done so much for me, and are such wonderful people to be around. Lou Manzi is another person who I am very close to. He used to own Dukes and Tots, both nightclubs 'rubber legs' attended in his dancing days! Peter Bryant has been a very close friend of mine over the years, and is one of the Four Musketeers. Another close friend, one of the Three Criers, is Steve Clow, my brilliant press agent and stunt manager.

Good friends are hard to find, so I have been really blessed. There's an old wartime saying, "Loose lips sink ships", which means a secret is no longer a secret when you tell somebody. Over the years, my friends have always trusted me. If I am told something, I will keep it a secret. I would never do anything to harm my relationships.

FUNDRAISING FOR CHARITY

I have helped to raise a lot of money for Chelmsford and the surrounding areas over the years. One night, we had an Elvis impersonator at a fundraising dinner and sold raffle prizes. I even recorded my favourite of the King's tunes, *The Wonder of You,* and sold it that night. We raised so much money that

25 years ago

ec 01 17 46 04 c

Local Elvis fans set for reunion

REMEMBER Elvis? The King of Rock and Roll who died on August 16, 1977, in Memphis, Tennessee, will never be forgotten by his millions of fans.

And hundreds of Essex followers will be gathering together at the Chancellor Hall, Chelmsford, next Thursday to pay tribute to the legendary 'Pelvis'.

The 'In Memory of Elvis' discotheque has been organised by Chelmsford business man Tony Appleton who saw the man himself on stage in Las Vegas in the seventies.

It is the third Elvis evening he has held in aid of charity and this time the money will be going towards a colour television for the children's ward at St John's Hospital, Chelmsford.

■ Were you at the In Memory of Elvis disco? Write and share your memories.

Forget Fortnum – make it Maldon

FORGET Fortnum and Mason's. Pass over Selfridges and take a look at the smart stores in your own home town.

That's the message from Maldon's recently-formed Chamber of Trade and Commerce, which is about to launch a "buy-it-in-Maldon" campaign.

Hundreds of publicity leaflets are currently being prepared for distribution not just to local homes but those further afield, in the bid to boost business.

Now or Never, Our Elvis Fundraising Night

125

evening, with the help of Angela Lodge, that we topped £6,000.

Another time we raised £8,000 for the Farleigh hospice. Afterwards, I won the Pride of Essex Award for achievement in Chelmsford, which they presented me with during a dinner. I thought they had invited me to be the Toastmaster for the event; I had no clue that I was going to get an award! They did me in like a kipper!

For twelve years, I also organised an evening disco at the old Chancellor Hall in Chelmsford, where we used to raise £1,000 a night for Guide Dogs for the Blind. A disabled man

Fundraising for Guide Dogs for the Blind

needed a scooter so we raised money for him too. I truly enjoy helping people. If you can do something to help, why not?

Another project that was a great success was a ladies' night ball for charity at the Ingatestone Masonic Lodge, where I was the Master. With the help of Angela Lodge of BBC Essex, we raised £4,250 for a permanent new Helen Rollason Cancer Support Centre in Chelmsford. The Support Centre now offers a range of therapies including reflexology, counselling, aromatherapy, manual lymphatic drainage and support groups.

MASONIC GENEROSITY

I have been a freemason for the past 25 years at my Lodge at Ingatestone. The Freemasons are the biggest fundraisers in the world, and my Lodge meet five times a year with the aim of helping hands. We try to help the next person who needs it, usually local people who need some money. A friend of mine had convinced me to join – Vernon Frost, a solicitor and an absolute hell raiser.

When I joined, the Lodge was ready to pack up, on its knees with only six members. After a while, I was voted in as the Master and turned it around. I went around Chelmsford, asking people to join, and we now have 40 members. During the meetings, you don't read out of books, it's all from memory. Every meeting we give money to a collection.

My life philosophy has always been to help other people. That's what the Freemasons are about; if anyone's in trouble you can go and help them out. Money has always been important to me, but not as important as good friends and a generous spirit. I make my own and look after my friends and myself.

NOW OR NEVER PART II

I am now racking my brain to think up ideas on how best to promote this autobiography. I could gate-crash the International Space Station, or I could recite it touring the UK on a hover board. Anything is possible for the Royalist Town Crier, but seriously I am hoping to organise some book-signing stunts across the galaxy somewhere, so watch out!

Well, it's been fun walking down memory lane with you and here's hoping I flog a few and raise money for the Helen Rollason charity. Who knows what life has in store for me, but I do look forward to writing my next book, 'Now Or Never Part 2'. You never know what the future holds, and you shouldn't worry about it anyways. As for me, I want to make more memories. I want to keep doing my thing by having fun and keeping forever young

WITH SPECIAL THANKS – IN ALPHABETICAL ORDER!

Alan Myatt, Alan Thomson, Alex Wilkinson, Angela Lodge, Dr Andrew Moore, Antonio Imperie, Dr Azmi Nadra, Carmel Walsh, Ciaran Gold, Craig the Gardener, Danny Manly, Dave Dennison, Dave Monk, Dipak Pau, Dusty Miller, Gerald Ford, Gill Jones, Gordon Shieds, Gordon West, Grant Cooper, Ivor Spencer, Jean-Louis Emmanuel Geurden and his receptionist Helen, John and Linda Hardy, Les Cooper, Lou Manzi, Malcolm Tilsed, Mark Day, Martin Day, Mel Baldwin, Mimosa Beauty, Pat Elmore, Paul Boits, Paul Dent-Jones, Peter Baker, Peter Bryant, Peter Minney, Peter Moore, Ray Bone, Robert, Lisa and Jason Bartella, Spin Thompson, Steve Clow, Susie Cornell MBE and Ian Cornell, Tom Corby MVO, Tony Pennack, Tony Bilton, Vernon Frost. Not forgetting all my loyal friends and those who have supported me over the years, and last but not least, Gemma Appleton, for her patience and professionalism in taking me back to the future. XXX

StoryTerrace®

Printed in Poland
by Amazon Fulfillment
Poland Sp. z o.o., Wrocław